ALSO BY THE AUTHORS

Angelspeake: How to Talk with Your Angels

The Angelspeake Book of Prayer and Healing

How to Work with Your Angels

Barbara Mark
&
Trudy Griswold

Simon & Schuster

SIMON & SCHUSTER
Rockefeller Center
1230 Avenue of the Americas
New York, NY 10020

SIMON & SCHUSTER and colophon are registered
trademarks of Simon & Schuster Inc.

ANGELSPEAKE is a registered trademark of
Barbara Mark and Trudy Griswold

Designed by Levavi & Levavi

Manufactured in the United States of America

10   9   8   7   6

Library of Congress Cataloging-in-Publication Data
Mark, Barbara.
The angelspeake book of prayer and healing : how to
work with your angels / Barbara Mark & Trudy Griswold.
p. cm.

1. Angels. 2. Prayer. 3. Spiritual life. I. Griswold, Trudy,
II. Title.
BL477.M363 1997
291.2' 15—dc21   97-27658
CIP
ISBN 978-1-4391-9106-4

Acknowledgments

There were many "angels" who helped us during the process of completing our second *Angelspeake* book.

There were "housing angels" who put us up (and who put up with us) as we traveled throughout the country. Thanks to Susan and Tom Carter, Carlos Laster, Molly Yowell, Laura Watson, Sue Storm, and Pat and Grigs Markham for the loan of their Vermont condo when we needed a place for isolated inspiration.

Thanks to the many "teaching angels" who have, in some way, taught us how to write a book or what to put in it: Geri Norrington, Millie Landis, Geneva Gorsuch, and Elizabeth Brown.

We have had plenty of "earth angels" who helped us with this book and throughout our lives, such as Jerry Mark, Gillian Drummond, Linda Engstrom, John Heise, Linda Engstrom, French Wallop, Virginia Callahan, Rabbi Judith Schindler,

Kathirswami, Bhuchung Tsering, Zak Chaudry, Celeste Kelley and Bryan Jameison.

Bless our "angel children," Caroline Griswold, Katie Griswold, Michael and Roema Mark, Suzanne Mark and her husband Joe Coco, and Stephanie and Monte Roberts. Thanks, kids, for the unconditional love with which you support us.

We thank our "angel sister," Jackie Anderson, and her daughters, Regan, Raena, and Rhyan. Thanks, girls, for being so fantastic to Aunt Trudy and Aunt Barbara.

Many "publishing angels" led us through from first word to The End. Our agents, John Sammis and Ron Jaffe, helped us clarify our message. Thanks to our Simon & Schuster support team who kept us on track: Dominick Anfuso and Holly Zappala, and Ana DeBevoise, who put together a million details and is the most organized person we know. And finally, a special thanks to Bob Griswold, editor extraordinaire, whose writing skills have always enhanced the message of *Angelspeake*. Thank you, Bob, for always saying "I'll do it."

All of the "encouragement angels" who know us, have hosted and attended classes, and have helped us through your cards, letters, phone calls, faxes, and e-mails, we thank you with all our being. By sharing your time and personal angel experiences with us, you have helped more people than you'll ever know.

And, of course, our "angel angels," John/Paul, Joshua, and Gabriel, who have helped us truly understand that life IS good. We are blessed.

This book is dedicated to
Chris Heise and Frank Smelik
and
to all who seek God through the angels . . .
on both sides of life.

Contents

11

Introduction

Life is good. When life feels bad, it is because we are not good in it. This is a book about having a good life. This book is about balance, reconciliation, and about tapping into the goodness life is.

God is good. God gives us life and God loves us. When we are apart from the goodness God *is*, when we try to run our life *our way*, then life becomes difficult. When we let life happen, when we surrender, when we reconcile with all the goodness God is, with the help of His angels, then life can be everything we decide to have it be. We can have a good life in spite of the most shattering event, the most dire trouble, fear, pain, or difficulty.

Life is not easy. Do not confuse good with easy. Our personal lives today are not easy, but they are very, very good. How can some people survive awesome difficulty, sickness, financial ruin, or death of loved ones, and rise to a place of serenity, understanding, and even joy? How can the most ruinous situation become the avenue to finding a good life? A great life? A life filled with peace? Can you do it? Can you turn your life into a joyful experience? Can you heal yourself and find a God who is loving and helpful? We say, yes, you can. The difference is having an enthusiastic and joyful attitude and a willingness to allow your angels to help you solve daily difficulties as they arise.

This book is about working *with* life. *Angelspeake* was about how to communicate with divine beings. This book is about how to use these same beings, once you have contacted them, in order to find a more joyful existence, to find a balance within yourself, and to form new attitudes toward yourself and God.

Life is good, and learning this truth is not going to be hard to do. God's angels are standing right beside you, as you read this line, waiting to help you. All you have to do is ask for their help, believe it will be given to you, let them help you, and then say thank you for the goodness that happens.

We know now that our angels didn't come to us because we were special, but rather because we were not. We know now that many other people are being "awakened" around the world. We also know we are no different from you, and thousands of others who are reading this book.

We have never seen an angel or been "plucked from the jaws of death." We are simply two sisters who, for some reason we may never fully know, were awakened by their angels. We were ready to listen when we first heard their message and we have continued to follow the guidance we have received from our angels every day since.

Angels help us in every way imaginable. They are messengers of God and do what God wants them to do. There is nothing they cannot do. At our first class we were asked, "Who do we pray to now that we know our angels?" The answer is God! God! God! When we pray, God responds through His angelic realm.

Over the years, we have formed a partnership with our angels and have found that our lives are happier, easier to manage, more abundant, and fulfilled. We have been taught by our angels, loved by them, led by them, but mostly, encouraged by them. What they told us would happen, has happened. Not always in the way we imagined. Usually better. From being full of doubt and skepticism, we have built a relationship of trust and friendship. We truly love our angels, feel their love in return, and cannot imagine our lives without them.

When we were opening to the angels and beginning to trust what they said to us, and did for us,

we went through a series of ups and downs emotionally, spiritually, intellectually, and personally. After our book *Angelspeake: How to Talk with Your Angels* was published, we began receiving many phone calls and letters from other seekers as they walked their spiritual path. We repeatedly heard one question: "What do I do now that I can communicate with my angels?"

You discovered that learning to Angelspeake was obviously only your first step in obtaining divine help. Now that you could communicate with angels, you wanted to move forward even faster, with more power and clarity. You longed to know more about angels and how to most effectively use their input in all areas of your life. Some of you had had great success with angelic communication, but not with letting your angels help you change your lives for the better.

A lot more was happening with students and readers around the world than we ever knew! The angels continued to teach us after *Angelspeake* was published. We learned that they were pleased with *Angelspeake,* and that people all over the world were reading it. Now it was time to deepen the message with another book. It was through hearing about your personal discoveries that we realized *The Angelspeake Book of Prayer and Healing* needed to be written. We began to be taught, as never before, the significance and importance of *The Four Fundamentals:* Ask, Believe, Let It Happen, and Say Thank You. We were already aware that these simple four directives could empower and change lives, but we had no idea how much or how encompassing those changes would be.

We see *Angelspeake* as the key to your communication with your angels. We see this book as the door to the storehouse of help your angels will give you to enjoy an enhanced, new, spiritual way of life. Use the lessons and encouragement of *Angelspeake* to improve your communication, and by all means, do your best to talk with your angels as often as you feel the need.

One of our first surprises came when *Angelspeake* appeared on the *Publishers Weekly* Religion Bestsellers List. We did not think of *Angelspeake* as a "religious" book! We looked at the book as a written form of our Angelspeake classes, and thought of it as a how-to book. Communications we received from our readers had nothing to do with religion either. Readers told us how writing to their angels had changed their lives.

Letters and phone calls related experience after experience of people writing to the angels and using *The Four Fundamentals.* We received letters from believers and doubters. We heard stories that bordered on the miraculous. We heard how people broke down their personal barriers and found freedom. We found people who built an "angel network" to give themselves and others needed support. We found some who had lifelong dreams come true. We found others who were saved from disaster—financial, spiritual, and physical. We found kindred spirits who had stories to share that taught us other ways to look at our own progress.

We found some angry and fearful people. We heard from a few so limited they could not believe anything except what was interpreted for them by others. We heard from people who had more concern for the world than they did for themselves and others who had never asked for anything for themselves in their entire lives! We found souls who could not pray and souls who could not stop praying. We heard from men who would not believe for fear they would have to give up their power if they became spiritual. We heard from women who were afraid to ask for themselves for fear the answer would lead them where they were afraid to go. Many, many tears were shed, sometimes long before we even said anything other than hello.

We received telephone calls from all over the world. We heard from friends with whom we had lost contact long ago. We received letters in languages we could not read. We were told *Angelspeake* had saved lives, changed lives, and opened lives. We were invited to bring our message to other parts of the country by doing seminars and workshops.

The Public Broadcasting System (PBS) filmed a workshop and affiliates began to air the program across the United States, spreading the *Angelspeake* message everywhere via television. The angels told us the message they gave us to teach would eventually become worldwide and we have seen that prophecy come true already.

We became aware that the book itself was only part of the *Angelspeake* experience. It seemed as though each book came with its own angel and that angel was specifically chosen for the reader. We heard from people who had found their book in the most amazing way, and we heard from people who bought ten or twelve at a time, to give to friends.

The message of *Angelspeake* is to learn to communicate with your angels in writing. *The*

Angelspeake Book of Prayer and Healing will help you create a new level of intimacy with your angels culminating in a lasting, healing, and personal union. Angel quotes will appear in colored italics to help you develop a better understanding of how angels communicate. *The Angelspeake Book of Prayer and Healing* begins where *Angelspeake* finished, appropriately, with a poetic overture from the angels.

Angel Touches

Think of a time when an idea came to you
that was so vivid and pure and was so true for you
rolls of shivers started in one part of your body and
then inundated every cell of your being.
You may call that
Angel touches or
Love rushes.
That was Us.
Think of a time when you awakened at night
with a thought so clear
you knew it answered your every question.
That was Us.
Think of a time when you were so still
you could hear
music and knew it was the "music of the spheres."
That was Us.
Think of a time when you loved so totally
you could not express it
for there were no words invented
to translate the feeling.
That was Us.
Think of a time when the earth,
and God,
and You

were so aligned that you knew it was your truth
in all its glory.
That was Us.
Think of peace so deep
you could not reach the bottom of it.
That was Us.
Think of a time you were so connected with love
and light
you said you were filled with God
or the Holy Spirit.
You were.
But it was also Us.
We are not hard to find.
We are there in the stillness.
We are there in the waiting.
We are there in the knowing.
Just BE.
We are there.

An Angel Prayer

Angels sent by God to guide me,
Be my light and walk beside me.
Be my guardian and protect me,
On the paths of life direct me.

Chapter 1

Everyone Can Angelspeake!

———◄✦►———

We began a spiritual journey when we were awakened by our angels. They asked us to write to them and to listen to their messages. Since then our lives and our view and understanding of the world have changed totally. When we were awakened, we were at a point in our lives when we were able to listen. For years, we had been seeking understanding in every corner. Perhaps we had been awakened many times before, but that day, we no longer had excuses. We were out of our own ideas. We were ready to hear.

From our first angelic communications, our lives began to change. One of the first important things we learned was to trust the messages we were receiving. We spent hours on the telephone trying to figure out what was coming to us, from whom, and why to us. We could not stop the messages from coming. We were being taught daily by the angels about God, the universe, love, and about our paths.

Before long we both began to receive messages specifically telling us to teach others how to speak with their angels. We asked for specific instruction, and said, "Angels, how does one learn the skill of writing to you?" The angels answered by teaching us what we now call The Seven Steps to

receive angel messages. These seven little techniques seemed so simple that at first we thought we had made them up. But, the more we thought of it, we realized that if we had made them up they would surely have been much more complicated, even intellectual! Our "humanness," as the angels would say, would have made sure of it! This is the angels' seven-step method, exactly as it was given to us when we asked them, "How does one learn to write to their angels?"

The Seven Steps to Talk with Your Angels

Practice, practice, practice, just as you have learned everything. Pray for guidance and insight. Remain open to the skill and allow it to come to you. Remember, all knowledge is already within you. All you need to do is access it. When you are learning, you are doing nothing more than remembering what you already know. Skill comes with repetition as in flying an airplane. You can already know how to fly an airplane in your brain; the skill comes through the practice of it. Knowledge will come to you in many ways—through study, through dreams, through experience. All will be there for you when you manifest the desire. In order to connect with the angels in writing, all you need to do is pray, breathe, listen, write, accept, follow your inner knowing, and trust.

1. **PRAY**. *Ask to receive clearly and to keep yourself out of it. Pray for the truth and gift of spiritual hearing. When you pray you are safely surrounded by God's love and protection. A favorite prayer is:*

   Angel of God my guardian dear,
   To whom God's love commits me here.
   Ever this day be at my side,
   To light and guard, to rule and guide.

2. **BREATHE**. *Sit and relax. Breathe and become open. Do not meditate. But also do not activate. Just be of serene nature.*

3. **LISTEN**. *The message comes to you as a whisper or may seem as your own thoughts, but it will stop and start. If you hear three words, type or write the three words. There may be a pause before the next words, but they will come. Do not force it.*

4. **WRITE**. *Hear the words come just a second*

before they are written. You will receive. Do not worry about them making sense. You do not have to go into some spiritual state. Just write what you hear as you hear it. Sometimes you will receive "thought sentences" where you know what you are going to write in total, like a story you know already or a phrase you frequently use. The harder you think, the less flow there will be.

5. **ACCEPT**. *What you write is what you write. The angels are guiding you, but it will feel as though you are making it up. It may always feel as though you are making it up. Acceptance is the most important part.*

6. **INNER KNOWING**. *There will be an absence of ego involved. You will not have to "think" about it or "plan" it as you would a paper. It just comes. You will find you don't remember what you wrote after you wrote it. It will always seem fresh.*

7. **TRUST.** *What the angels tell you is the best information they have at the time you receive it. Angels will not run your life. This is a guidance to speed you along and teach you skills you will need in your life's work. These are spiritual gifts. You did not have to do anything to get them. More will be given to you as you progress. Do not dissect for accuracy. Free will and different*

timetables create different patterns similar to ocean currents. It is possible to predict where they are going, but not possible to control them or to predict accurately.

Angels are always working for your highest good. Feel free to ask questions and, if you want to, ask for the angel's name who is writing to you. Everyone has a guardian angel, but also there are many other angels who will come to you as you need specific help or attention. Expect different personalities, energies, interests, and knowledge levels. Some angels are extremely wise and intelligent. Others are sent to bring you joy and love. There are angels for every need.

LINDA H.'S STORY:

I was in Colorado in a situation that needed changing right then! I believe in asking the angels for help, but I needed immediate results. I read in *Angelspeake,* "Ask and Be Specific," so I was. Here is some of what happened.

1. I wrote: "Angels of Employment, I need a good job in Ohio near my children with perfect pay and location." One week later, I had it all.

2. I wrote: "Angels of Houses and Rentals, I need a house in a good location, okay for pets, available immediately, at the lowest possible fair price." In five days, I had a lovely duplex, ten minutes from my job.

3. I wrote: "Angels of Movers, I need a mover, *very reasonable and immediately!*" I was led to an independent company owned by a man named Mike. With only a week's notice, Mike's company moved all my belongings from Colorado to Ohio. My new boss paid the movers and let me pay her back by payroll deduction.

4. I wrote: "Angels of State License Plate Issues, HELP ME!" I did not have $250 for a car tax I needed to pay. A helpful man at the title bureau listened to my story, gave me the number of another person, and said, "Call this man. He really helps people out." The next day, a high-ranking state official

called and loaned me—a perfect stranger—the money for the tax.

Thank you angels! And thank you Barbara and Trudy for all your help. May the "Angels of Great Book Days" be with you.

There are many divine teachers assigned by God, other than angels, archangels, and guardian angels, to work with you. Some are known as masters, teachers, or spirit guides who once may have lived on earth, but are now back in spirit and have accepted the duties of healing, teaching, or helping those of us still living on earth. We refer to all of these spiritual beings who may come through in a communication as angels, although technically speaking, many reserve the term "angels" exclusively for divine beings who have never been "in body." Often you will not know, without asking, which type of being is speaking through this form of "automatic dictation." Just know that the highest being necessary for the message to get through is the one who is giving it.

You may also find that someone you knew or loved and who has died may come to you in a loving way. You may experience them through a clear message, a sense of presence, their chosen fragrance, or even a touch on your cheek or shoulder. Spouses, grandparents, parents, and friends may come to you.

No one is too young or too old to contact their angels for their supportive and loving messages. One of our students introduced the angels at her family reunion.

LIZ'S STORY:

When I went home to visit my family, I took my angel notebook in order to share my angel messages. Everyone wanted to write their own angels, so I taught them Angelspeake's simple principles. We were a diverse group, the oldest being my father, who was eighty-six, down to my nephew, who was twelve. After we said a prayer, everyone started writing. It looked to me as though my father and brother were "planning" what to write and I thought they weren't going to get anything, but when they read their first message, they wept as they read the beautiful words they had received. I was amazed!

My nephew's message from his angel was particularly enlightening. He read, "Don't let the bullies at school make you nervous." His mother, who was also there said, "What bullies?" She had no idea her son was being tormented at school!

The entire experience brought all of us to a greater understanding of each other. I am always amazed by the messages and how simple it is to "tune in." I feel I have my best friends with me, always ready to be a loving support, a guiding light gently prodding me to keep moving, and to lighten up! Everyone benefits from "angel speaking."

···━━━···

AN ANGEL MESSAGE:

Dearest Children,

We are always with you, but we can help you so very much more when you ask us to come to you for specific help. If you are wondering what to do next to further your spiritual quest and to find your path, we can only say this. Talk to us. Talk to us. Talk to us. We listen and will answer. Believe it.

A Muslim Call to Prayer

I stand in witness to the fact that
there is no God except one.
I stand in witness to the fact
that Muhammad
(peace be on him) is Allah's
messenger.

Chapter 2

You, God, and Your Angels

Teaching people how to Angelspeake was the easy part. During our classes, we began to see that once students learned to open the doors to their angels, they needed to know how to relate to the angels in a way they could understand. What were they to do with their new angel friends? How were they to work together?

To help us work with them, the angels taught us *The Four Fundamentals:* Ask, Believe, Let It Happen, and Say Thank You. At first we thought *The Four Fundamentals* were just a simple method of asking angels for their help when it was needed.

We were not interested in asking for much more than finding parking places, or help in recovering lost objects, or for their help in bringing a few material possessions into our lives. Instead, these four little rules have become the foundation of our spiritual life. They have not only taught us how to connect with the angelic realm but also how to incorporate greater joy, peace, and self-assurance into each aspect of our lives.

We have learned to use Ask, Believe, Let It Happen, and Say Thank You to help us with anything we want to have, to be, or to do. Here are *The Four Fundamentals* and how the angels have instructed us to use them.

The Four Fundamentals

1. **ASK** and be specific in your request. Asking invites the angels to come to you and clarifies what you want them to do.
2. **BELIEVE** and trust that if what you are asking for is the right thing for you, then it will happen in the right way at the right time.
3. **LET IT HAPPEN**. Allow the angels to do their work. Expect positive results.

4. **SAY THANK YOU.** Complete the communication with words of gratitude.

Your Life and You

At some point in your life you are probably going to ask yourself, *"What is next?"* You may have become a seeker, without really knowing what it is you are seeking. You may have a sense of approaching change, without knowing specifically what it is that needs to be changed. You may begin to recognize that your thoughts and feelings are dominated by the belief that there is *"something"* out there for you to do, but you know neither what it is nor how to find it, and are fearful you will miss the important *"something,"* without ever knowing what it was that you missed!

Our major task as human beings is to keep our balance, to maintain our focus on what is truly most important while juggling all the physical, emotional, and even spiritual pressures we face. Our lives are designed to function best as an *equilateral triangle,* a triangle with three equal sides and identical angles. The geometry of the equilateral triangle gives it enormous strength. Imagine *your* life as an equilateral triangle. Label one side of the triangle **body,** another side **mind,** and the last side **spirit.** If you shorten one side or reduce one angle, you lose the structural integrity of the triangle.

Why is stability of body, mind, and spirit so important? We want balance so the highs don't get too high and the lows don't get too low during the day-to-day acts of living. It is how we look at life that colors the understanding of the messages we receive from the angels.

Angels speak from the highest levels. The more we keep our mind filled with positive and loving thoughts, the easier our life becomes. When we choose to keep our thoughts on lower levels, at the very least we experience unnecessary daily struggle, but even worse we may miss the entire point of life itself.

Barbara talks about how she used to wake up in the morning knowing that there was a "bowling ball" of fear hanging over her, and the more awake she became, the more she would feel the fear come toward her. By the time she was fully awake, the ball had fallen *into* her chest and she knew she would have to breathe and swallow around it all day long. Fear filled her life to the point she felt it physically.

By contrast, Trudy carried her fear in her stomach as a nauseous lump. She tried to melt that lump by running harder and faster all day long. She thought that the more perfectly she did her daily tasks the more she could chip away at the horrid lump. Trudy tried control—thinking the more control she maintained over life's events and the people around her, the better she would feel. She ran so hard, perfected every task, and controlled every situation only to fall into bed exhausted, sleep fitfully, and awaken with the ever-present nauseous lump still there. Trudy became a "human doing" rather than a human being.

Fear doesn't run our lives any longer. The day is the day and the events are what happen throughout the day. Days are neither good nor bad. The day simply *IS*. Each one presents a new perspective, not a new scorecard. We believe sleep is a divine gift that presents us with an opportunity to start new and refreshed every twenty-four hours.

The usual order of the words "body," "mind," and "spirit" indicates where the priorities of most people exist: first, body; second, mind; third, spirit. Is it possible that we have been living life upside down by giving body and mind top priority over spirit? Ask yourself this question: Am I a physical person having a spiritual (and intellectual) experience, or am I really a spiritual being currently having a physical experience?

Beginning in the hospital nursery, and ever since, we have been doted over physically by family and friends. Our body is most obvious to us. We feed, pamper, exercise, decorate, and criticize it, and we spend endless amounts of money and time trying to improve it.

As we become adults we begin to focus on our minds. We not only seek knowledge of all kinds and skills to maintain a job, we also begin to look for "peace of mind." We read the latest books, try new forms of meditation, and listen to audiotapes. We believe that by keeping our bodies running at peak performance and our minds maintaining the right attitudes, then peace of mind will be ours.

The real dilemma is this: When we work *only* on our bodies and minds to seek perfection and ignore our spirituality, happiness becomes more and more elusive. We become more out of balance and further from the very balanced state we seek.

Our spiritual side is the one area of our life we least look at and nurture, yet it is the most important. If our spirit is healthy, if we love ourselves,

43

and if we love God, we will love our minds and bodies also. Spirit is really our first priority and when that is our belief, our attitudes toward mind and body will be healthy, too, and will effortlessly fall into place.

In other words, our lives are designed to be developed three-dimensionally, spirit, body, mind. Our responsibility is to maintain the balance.

This book is about strengthening the spiritual side of our triangle. When we focus on our body or mind, we are concerned with how we look, or how we measure up to others. Focusing on our spirit is about how we relate to *ourselves!*

In every class and during nearly every private appointment we are asked, "What am I supposed to do with my life?" or, "What is my path?" Material possessions and achievements have proven not to be enough. People are not fulfilled and they want to know what's missing.

When we begin to ask such questions relating to our spiritual side, and then seek real answers to such questions, conflicts are inevitable. Let's face it, most of us have undeveloped, adult "spirit sides." We haven't invested time or energy in this area. We look for spiritual understanding, and we long to know God better, but our past personal experience with God more than likely has been unsatisfactory. Now we realize we have to first deal with our confused and questionable relationship with Him.

Your Life and God

Trudy described a recent, particularly doubting class composed of students who asked endless questions about *The Four Fundamentals.* "Finally, I asked them to write down three reasons why they would find it difficult to use these fundamentals which we had found to be extremely helpful. I was amazed to realize that my simple question about why people couldn't use *The Four Fundamentals* became a huge discussion on why they didn't believe God would answer their prayers." Together, with the responses of others in many classes, we uncovered some amazing beliefs and surprising opinions which prevented many students from accepting what God could do for them.

We began to ask members of each class several questions. First: "Do you find it difficult to use

The Four Fundamentals, and if so, why?" We discovered that nearly every class member was distrustful of any kind of contact with God.

Next, we asked: "Why can't you ask God for help?" The response was startling and was summed up by one student's four-word answer, "I don't deserve it!" There were some who had a mature, secure relationship with God, but a surprisingly high number held the view that God and His angels might work for *others* but certainly not for them!

We found it hard to get people to ask God for help. Most didn't believe they were worthy of gifts from God or the angels. There was a pervasive thought that whatever you had in life *now* was what you were stuck with forever. Some students were embarrassed to ask for anything for themselves while also being fearful that if they received a gift, they might misuse it. Others feared that God kept a gift "scorecard." If he gave you something, you had better use it wisely!

We learned that people believed in God, but they did not believe that God believed in them! Some were almost fearful that God would actually notice them. They lived in fear, believing it was better to lie low and maybe God wouldn't bother them with anything—good or bad!

God has received so much bad publicity that it's no wonder so many people are afraid of Him. From our earliest years we have been taught to fear Him. We have been told He is angry and that we are sinners, and as sinners we are not worthy of Him. Furthermore, God punished "sinners." He kicked Adam and Eve out of the Garden of Eden for making one mistake. Despite good and noble efforts, religion's attempts to teach us to honor God has too often taught us to fear Him.

Bryan J. illustrates. "When I was a boy, and saw terrible things happen to people, I was told, 'God works in strange ways. We cannot question the will of God.' Everyone seemed to blame God for catastrophes. But later when I was grown and bought a 25-cent chance on a brand-new automobile—and won it—everyone said, 'Wow, are you lucky!' It seemed to me, God always was blamed for the bad stuff but never was given credit for the good stuff."

Every once in a while someone says, "God loves you like a father," with no thought that very few of us had fathers who were admirable role models. As much as we loved our own father, he was certainly not God-like!

Our continuing survey uncovered a broadly based and deep-seated distrust of anything divine working personally for anyone. We found that people retained their childlike values and injected them into their adult belief system. One woman even told us she thought of God as the ultimate abusive parent and was scared to death of what He might do. Ultimately we found seven different reasons why people could not relate to God, reasons which had become deep-rooted and enduring. As you read them, ask yourself which beliefs you may hold.

Why People Don't Ask God for Help

- I have been taught asking for anything for myself is selfish.
- I might get what I want and then have to "deal" with it.
- I might pray or ask wrong, or ask for the wrong thing in the wrong way.
- Prayer didn't work for me before! God doesn't hear me.
- Material things are evil or bad. Rich people don't get to heaven.
- If I get "good" things I'll also have to take "bad" things.
- I don't deserve anything.

Our angels tell us that God has a plan for us and while we are here on earth we are on a continual road to discovery. Yet, we find that few people look at themselves as being part of a divine process. Many think, "God is up there somewhere and I am down here and unimportant."

We help our students realize that angels only do God's will and that God is truly a loving, caring God. God and the angels are *both* part of each person's spiritual process and fit together. When

most people realize they are opening their "door" to spirituality, and that includes getting to know God, they experience the beginning of spiritual growth for which they have longed, and their spiritual side begins to grow rapidly.

The third side of the triangle, spirit, was an enormous vacuum for so many. We had all these spiritual seekers coming to our classes and they didn't even believe they were part of God's plan at all. Our challenge was to help them reconnect to God and heal their relationship with Him so they could grow themselves.

All we wanted to do was teach people how to communicate with their angels, and now we were into a whole God-concept arena. Living a spiritual life meant more than writing to the angels and receiving a reply. It also meant having to learn to understand the information we obtained. It was time for all of us to look at our convictions in order to find out how they relate to our own personal experiences. Whether we were eager or not, we were going to get the opportunity to work on being balanced, on experiencing the structural strength of the equilateral triangle, balancing body, mind—and now spirit.

Your Life and the Angels

Thank you, God, for angels! It has been through the angelic realm that we have been able to approach a once frightening God and begin to see Him as a good guy for the first time. The angels talk so highly of God! They tell us how much He loves us and how He helps us and how we are to ask for what we need from Him. They constantly teach us how to relate to God.

We believe one reason God sent the angels to earth was to help us come back to Him in a way we can deal with. We can make up with God through our angels, without fear of punishment of any kind. The anxiety we felt when dealing with

God isn't present when we talk with our angels.

Angels have been depicted as loving, kind, and helpful. We are told angels bring sweet dreams and protect us from the bogeyman. Artists show angels as beautiful and comforting. We are told they bring good news and are considered accessible and trustworthy. God is usually depicted as masculine and punishing. Angels are shown as feminine and friendly.

No matter where our level of faith, our inner longing is leading us right back to God. In spite of any fear we continue to hold of Him, we cannot escape the attraction He holds for us. We long to reunite with Him.

Our soul, we are told, *is* God. So if we deny Him, we deny ourselves. Perhaps the path we are seeking so diligently *is* the third side of the triangle. It is our own spirituality that we are longing to find.

JUDY'S STORY:

I have suffered from chronic depression and fatigue for over forty-four years. The doctors say it is a chemical imbalance in the brain, but it is very frightening and frustrating when you have no control over your thoughts, feelings, and words. I was prescribed *every* antidepressant, but nothing seemed to work and I began to think my family would be better off if I was dead. Eventually, I ended up in the psychiatric ward. I am not sorry or ashamed I was put there because it was the best and safest place for me to be, but at the time, I was scared to death!

I have always had a strong faith and belief in God and my angels. The help I received from them is why I am still alive today. When I wanted to drive off a cliff, I heard, *You don't really want to do that,* and I answered, "Yes, I do! I want the suffering to end!"

Things were very rough for a long time. My husband had been disabled for many years. I had two kids to raise (one with a learning disability). I had problems with my daughter, problems with our landlady, car troubles, money troubles, and on and on. I was the major breadwinner when I was laid off from a job I had held for more than fourteen years. "Now what?" I asked.

Well, guess what? I had a complete nervous breakdown. This is what I had to do to get myself to *stop* what I was doing. I finally had to give up trying to run my own life and I asked for help from God. He led me to some wonderful teachers who I call my "earth angels" because they loved me until I was able to love myself again.

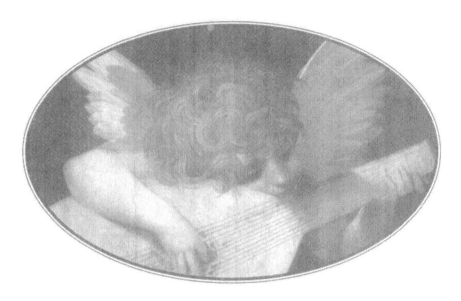

I knew I needed healing, and I was led to become a healer. Through classes I took in healing techniques, I learned to heal myself, and when I was healed, joy was free to enter my life. I never thought I was worthy of health, happiness, or abundance, so I didn't have them. Today I believe I am worthy of all the goodness God has to offer and so I have it.

I still have challenges to overcome and lessons to learn, but I know my angels are always with me with their unconditional love. Thanks to their guidance, I know I have a mission in life and I know what that mission is. The healer has been healed.

My advice to you is: do what you need to do to help yourself. But most of all, *Ask* your angels for help. *Believe* they are helping and will continue to help you. *Let Go* because you don't have to do it by yourself. And then, *Say Thank You* for their love, even if you don't feel their help at the time. They are there for you, but you have to invite them into your heart and into your life.

AN ANGEL MESSAGE:

Dear Children of God,

God is Balance and Law. The laws of the universe restore balance when it is awry, and bring balance where it has never been. Each of you was balanced when you entered the earth. As a babe, you had needs to eat, sleep, and be clean. You desired balance of the body. Soon you wanted to learn about the world you had entered, and as your mind became engaged you added the need for balance of your mind. When did you learn balance for your spiritual nature? Children, you always had it. All you are doing now is trying to remember it. We will help you.

A Hindu Prayer

O Divine Beings of all three
worlds,
We meditate upon the glorious
splendor
of the Vivifier Divine. May
He Himself
illumine our minds.

56

Chapter 3

Breaking Down Barriers

Freedom Through The Four Fundamentals

Ihe *Four Fundamentals* were meant to help us get out of our own way, but they also seemed to be full of barriers to progressing spiritually. We wanted to teach they were the *key* to progress. The angels had told us that when we learned to Ask, Believe, Let It Happen, and Say Thank You our personal barriers would drop and we would become more focused.

Learning to Ask

God gave each of us the gift of Free Will in order to run our lives. We have been given the ability to make our own decisions and choices. When we ask, we are allowing the angels to help us.

Asking is simply telling the angels what you would like to be, to do, or to have. Then ask for their help to receive it without complicating your request. It is easy to ask for simple things. It is easy to believe we are worthy of a convenient parking space. But when we elevate our requests to what we consider expensive, difficult, or even impossible, our old belief system overtakes us, our feeling of unworthiness surfaces, and we feel stuck and full of doubt. We asked the angels, "How can we solve this dilemma?" Here is what they taught us:

First, there are three major categories of Asking for what you want.

1. **To Be:** Asking for help in achieving a personal goal. "Angels, help me be more honest."
2. **To Do:** Asking for help in an activity. "Angels, please help me get into medical school."

3. **To Have:** Asking for a particular item or event. "Angels, please help me find a new apartment."

Second, be specific about whatever you want to be, to do, or to have. Write down your request or say it out loud. Visualize it. Experience receiving it and enjoying it. Create a clear mental picture of your request being fulfilled. This is the time to be as clear as possible, not only in what you are asking for, but in being it, doing it, and having it. Act as if it is already accomplished.

The Challenges of Asking

If you believe you are not worthy to receive something you asked for, or that God does not like you or hear you, it is going to be difficult to ask for anything you need or want, expecting that you will receive it. It will be difficult, but not impossible. Do it anyway. Asking is not about you. It is about opening to the goodness God has in store for you.

Asking brings change. Many of us fear change, even while we are looking everywhere for it. We want a better job, but don't want to leave the one we have. We hate our relationship, but are not willing to be alone, even for a moment. We can't

stand our home, but are too comfortable to move. We can't have it both ways. If nothing changes, nothing changes.

STUDENT QUESTIONS WITH ANGEL ANSWERS:

Q. I expect God and the angels to know what I want and is best for me.

Asking is the invitation for angels to go to work for you. Unless you ask, we can't help. You have

*free will to make choices. We do not know what
you have chosen unless you tell us.*

Q. I would feel selfish asking for material things.

*Ask anyway. It is never selfish or impolite to
treat yourself lovingly. If you do not ask for yourself, you will never learn how good angels are and
how much we love you.*

Learning to Believe

Under God's direction, the angels will bring what
you ask for if it is for your greater good. You will
not receive harmful gifts from your angels. Believe
that what you have asked for is already yours. Then
believe that God, through His angels, will bring it
to you and that you are worthy of receiving what
you have asked for.

Some Barriers to Believing

Once you have asked expectantly, as though your
request had already been granted, there are *no*
barriers. The only doubts will come from your
own ideas of yourself or from your self-limiting

beliefs. Your self-esteem will affect your ability to believe. For example, if you believe you are unworthy to have what you asked for, it is unlikely that you will receive it. In the Christian Bible, James 4:2 tells us, *"You have not because you ask not."* We don't have what we want simply because we did not ask! Ideally, our self-esteem should have nothing to do with either our request or our reception of that for which we have asked. But, unfortunately, low self-esteem often inhibits our ability to ask, but even to a greater extent, our ability to believe we will receive. Neither asking nor believing is about you, but rather about all that God has to give you.

Different requests may represent different values. For example, you may value your job and easily be able to ask for a promotion and believe it will be yours. However, at the same time you may not highly value owning a new car and feel uncomfortable or unworthy about owning a nice vehicle. Asking and Believing are separate, fundamental actions. They are both part of the divine plan through which God provides for us. Self-esteem is the deciding factor as to what you are able to ask for and what you believe you can receive.

We have a dear, close friend who is a powerful, professional businesswoman capable of negotiating her position in any business arena. However, in her personal relationship, she is unable to ask for and receive any respect whatsoever from her partner. This person has good self-esteem in business life, counterbalanced by a very low level of self-worth in love relationships. Such dichotomies are not rare.

Asking involves expectancy. Believing involves trust. Combined, they permit you to demonstrate your trust in God's goodness. Then you can allow yourself to receive any of God's gifts.

JUDITH'S STORY:

Angels make life safer and more fun. I used to test and look for external validation that they were real. I wanted to make sure that I was not, 1) crazy, 2) fooling myself, or 3) talking to myself. The problem was that I didn't trust my awareness.

The book *To Hear the Angels Sing* by Dorothy Maclean had a big effect on me and helped me be open to the idea that I could "listen" to the angels of plants and creatures. I had an herb garden that was not doing well in the Texas heat. I was tuning into a comfrey plant which looked as if it were dead. I was about to throw it out when I heard my angel say, "Take a soaking washcloth and lay it on top of the plant. Leave it there." I felt foolish doing it, but three days later when I lifted the washcloth, there was one tiny green leaf beginning to grow. The plant did not die. I was beginning to trust the messages I was receiving.

One time, my car broke down and I was stranded a long way from home. I called a friend who was a great mechanic, but he couldn't figure out what was wrong with the car. The angels showed me there was a little wire inside the engine that had melted and had caused a short in the electrical system. When I finally got the nerve to tell the mechanic what I was being told was wrong, he fixed it with just a little piece of electrical tape.

Looking back, I realize these lessons were not about a dead plant or a broken vehicle. I needed to learn to trust my "knowing" and my angels. Sometimes I feel uncomfortable and foolish doing some of the things I "know" to do, but then I remember that my life is not out of control, it is just out of *my* control, which is a wonderful knowing!

What your family believed will influence what you believe. If your family believed that being relatively poor was Godly and being very wealthy was sinful, you may carry some or all of that belief "baggage." What we were taught as children is often part of what limits us as adults. You're a grown-up now. Be courageous and outrageous! Practice asking for things that are outside your comfort zone.

People say, "I'll believe it when I see it."

Angels say, "You'll see it when you believe it."

STUDENT QUESTIONS WITH ANGEL ANSWERS:

Q. I can't believe the angels want to talk to me.

You are as worthy as any being in God's universe. We will bring you what is right for you. We are always there for you.

Q. Believing is fine for others. But I feel blocked and simply can't believe.

Do not be afraid. God never asks you to change or move forward without a support system around you. You will not be alone during a time of change or growth. Are you willing to release the block, knowing that we will always be there with you? You can move beyond your comfort zone. That is what we call growth.

Learning to Let It Happen

Allow what you have asked for to come to you and believe you will receive. Be open, receptive, and patient. Don't get in the way. Let go of controlling the outcome. Trust divine methods. Wonderful things are going on that you know nothing about and the best is yet to be.

DEVELOPING PATIENCE

We have been taught we must *do something* if we want results. It is not a human trait to allow events to happen in the events' own good time. You do not have to do anything to hurry or rush the process when divine beings are aiding you. Do not fix or manipulate the outcome. It is not necessary to keep asking, praying, or begging. Allow. Allow. Allow. Be still and know that God has received your request and is working on it. You have not been forgotten.

STUDENT QUESTIONS WITH ANGEL ANSWERS:

Q. I can't give up my power to anyone, even my angels.

The power you hold so dear, child, is really stubbornness born of a need to believe in yourself. Letting go is not relinquishing power, it is trusting the God of the universe to work on your problem. The first thing is to ask. Keep asking for help to ask.

Q. I have to earn what I ask for.

God sends no bill. If you need to pay for what God gives you, then feed the hungry, kiss a child, do the laundry for your family. You may give what is not required, but why? Love expects no payment.

Q. I am afraid my life will change too drastically if I use these fundamentals.

Let Go and Let God, is a way to Let It Happen.

You are seeking the meaning of your life, and instead of allowing it to come to you, you are scrambling about looking here and there for what is right before you. Be still. God will bring you all you need or want if you Let It Happen.

Learning to Say Thank You

All God expects from you for any of your requests is a thank-you. Nothing else. When you say thank you, the angels are kept in the front of your mind and you notice the goodness available everywhere. You stay connected to the source of all you will ever need and will receive.

DEVELOPING GRATITUDE

If you are feeling apathetic, afraid, or angry, a gratitude list will help you see the beauty in the world. Every night, just before you go to bed, make a list of the things you are grateful for that happened during the day. The only rule is, try to include at least five things on your list. You may be grateful for a phone call from an old friend, for seeing a beautiful sunset, enjoying a baby's smile, for finding a bargain at the store, or receiving a C on a test

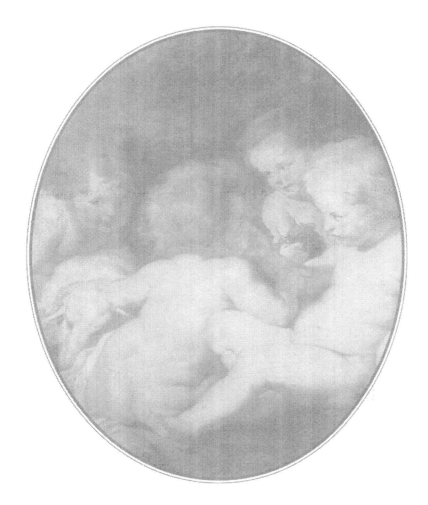

on which you thought you did poorly. It is fun to find unexpected gifts from God each day.

Soon, you will find you are seeing the world through different eyes. You begin to *look* for things to be grateful for. You stop being so self-centered and become more aware of the good things in your life. You begin to see yourself as part of a bigger picture. You see yourself as being a part of God's world.

STUDENT QUESTIONS WITH ANGEL ANSWERS:

Q. I felt terrible because I got what I asked for and then I didn't want it.

This is a sign of your growth of spirit. You no longer required what you thought you did because you had advanced so much. No gift is ever wasted. The gift will end up in its proper place.

Q. If I do all this, maybe I'll get too much good stuff.

Wonderful! Then you may give your surplus to those who have nothing. Be sure to ask for a great deal and the strength to deliver it where it is needed. For then you will be doing the work of God, who gives to those who ask, believe, let it happen, and say thank you. If you get too much "good stuff," then the fundamentals have worked. Pass it on! Do not decide for God what is too much. Only God knows how much is too much. There is no such thing as Too Much. There is only fear of abundance.

KATIE D.'S STORY:

My angel's name is KJS and he tells me many angels have names with no vowels. I know he is real by some of the things that have happened to me.

I am a doctoral student and an administrator at a local college. With less than a year of work left to complete my doctorate, I was at the end of my financial and inspirational resources. I particularly needed more time to write my dissertation and more money to buy some important and expensive support materials to complete my work. Fi-nan-cial Aid had turned down my last several requests for money, and if I took time off from my job to do the required writ-ing, I wouldn't have an income to support myself. I was sure I wasn't going to be able to make it by the deadline. Then KJS told me to call the authors of *Angelspeake.*

Since I am from California, I called Barbara. When I reached her, I was frantic. I told her all about my frustrations and how my dreams were going down the tube. She said, "Slow down and let go of wanting your doctorate!" How could I do that? But, step by step she took me through Asking, Believing, and Letting Go. She showed me how to "breathe" all my anxieties away, and after I did that, I wasn't afraid anymore. I let go of wanting money to live on and for project costs. I let go of wanting more time, wanting the expensive support material, and wanting a printer for my computer. I even let go of wanting approval from the committee who had to approve of my proposal and hear my oral examination.

When I started letting go and asking my angels for assistance, it was as though I started a miraculous series of events. What had been big blockages became open doors. I asked my boss for two days a week leave *with pay.* It was granted! I asked for a laser printer and within hours one was loaned to me. I asked for all I needed and every concern was cleared away easily. When I told my mother how everything was going, but I was still worried about funding, she said, "I can give you what you need." She told me it would be my parents' way of supporting me. It was a wonderful surprise!

KJS told me, *You need many signs to show you we are really there to help you. Our love often comes in the form of gifts. We want you to be successful and happy, child.*

I am now finishing my doctorate, enjoying the process in serenity and without fear. In just one week, with angelic guidance, my walls came down and I am in sight of my Ph.D. Thanks KJS!

AN ANGEL MESSAGE:

The importance of The Four Fundamentals in your life cannot be overstated. If you do not have one request to make for yourself, then make requests for those who cannot make them for themselves. Ask for the ability to feed those who are hungry. Ask for a way to help the homeless. Ask for coats so you can give them to those who are cold. Ask for healing for the sick children. Ask for a peaceful transition for those who are dying. Ask for world peace, and ask for yourself—for the knowledge of God's will for you, and the power to carry it out. There is plenty to ask for. Believe it.

The Serenity Prayer

God, Grant me the Serenity

To Accept the things

I cannot change,

The Courage to change

the things I can,

And the Wisdom to know

the difference.

Chapter 4

About Prayer

Deciding What to Be, Do, or Have

By now you have recognized if you have difficulties relating to God, therefore slowing your spiritual progress. You have a clear sense of the need for balance in body, mind, and spirit. It is time now to focus on *you* and find out what you want to be, to do, or to have in your life.

We teach our students to recognize the areas in their lives that need to be strengthened. The areas relate to actual behavior, not opinions. By focusing on these areas you will clearly see where you are inhibiting your spiritual growth and maturity and where you lack self-esteem. Once you identify the areas which block your growth, the angels will help you work your way through them.

Let's begin with a look at the Balance Wheel below. Each spoke represents an important aspect of your life. Using a scale of one to five (with five being highest) place a mark on each spoke indicating your current performance in each part. We suggest you look at these particular areas of your life to start.

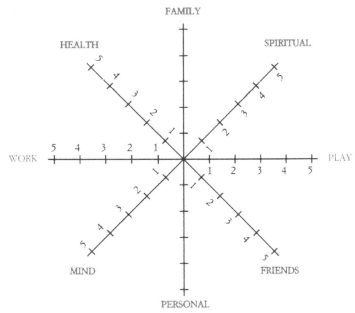

Rate yourself in each area:
5 = Excellent; 4 = Good; 3 = Average;
2 = Needs improvement; 1 = Poor

Personal. If you feel you give yourself adequate time each day for reflection, privacy, and something that gives you particular joy, you will probably want to mark the spoke between three and five. On the other hand, if you have little or no time for yourself and constantly put the needs of others ahead of your own, your score will likely be very much lower.

Mind. Are you studying something new and expanding your interests? When was the last time you read a book? How much time are you spending watching TV?

Work. Does your life center around your job to the exclusion of every other area? Are you working weekends and nights? Do you hold down more than one job? Or, conversely, have you been out of work or are you in a job you hate?

Health. How much do you exercise? Are you too fat or too thin? Do you have energy and pep? Are you getting adequate rest?

Family. Are you saving time for those you care about the most or are you too busy spending time in other areas?

Spiritual. Are there times set aside in your life to reflect and pray? Do you feel close to God or far away from Him? How often do you speak to your angels?

Play. Where does fun come into your life? Do you participate in a group or skill you enjoy for no other reason than you like to do it?

Friends. Do you spend time with people you enjoy being with, doing things you mutually like to do? Do you desire more or better friendships?

You may have other categories in your life we did not mention. School, love relationships, children, and so on are all important spokes you may wish to add.

Now, connect the marks with a continuous line into a "circle." Once the dots are connected, the "circle" may have an irregular shape. If you have a nicely balanced "wheel of life," congratulate yourself for your hard work. On the other hand, if your wheel resembles a flat tire, you know where to begin work to bring your life into the best possible balance.

Your wheel may be reasonably round, but with low numbers on each spoke. For example, you may have scored yourself one or two in each area. While your wheel may not be a "flat tire" it may not be fully inflated either. In this case, you may want to address your overall quality of life. By raising the level of joy in each area you will maintain your balance and experience a greater sense of purpose and happiness.

This simple, self-administered view of your areas of highs and lows has identified both the areas of importance in which you excel and the areas of importance you may want to improve. With what you have learned, you can ask your angels for guidance. Here are some thought starters:

How can I raise the quality of my life?
How can I find more time for play?
Where can I meet a spiritual buddy?
What can I read to challenge my mind?
What can I do to improve my health?

What can I do to unite my family?
How can I stop working *all the time?*
How can I bring more friends to my life?

We were able to work with God and the angels when we saw where we needed help. We became partners with the divine realm and worked with them daily to solve problems. When fear and trouble began to creep into our lives, we checked our balance wheels. Usually our trouble had something to do with one of our lower areas. We looked at where *we* were out of balance rather than asking why *God* had abandoned us. We quit blaming God for why our lives weren't working, and our angels helped us see we were not God's victim, but that we had control over our own lives. Believe us, that was empowering.

Once you have found the areas of your life in which you are deficient or where you are sabotaging yourself, you will better understand fully how asking specifically for what you want *to be, to do,* or *to have* is important. In spite of personal blocks which have been stopping you, you will be able to receive all the help God and the angels have to offer and will progress much more quickly.

But then you ask: "What *is* in the future? Where *am* I going? How do I begin living the life

I have always wanted?" Begin at the beginning. Look at where you are today.

For example:

To Be: What is your heart's desire? What is your most outrageous thought of what you could ever think to aspire to? When you were young, what did all those people say that you couldn't do because you weren't smart enough, good enough, or healthy enough? What is in the core of you that *you* know you can be, that *you* can do, and that *you* can have? Perhaps you have never even said your desire out loud because it sounded silly.

To Do: What is there in your being that you love to do so much, you would do it for free? What do you love so much that you would stay up all night to do it? What experiences of your life do you tell stories about? What do you think about in your private moments? What can't you wait to get home from work to do?

To Have: What do you frequently dream about having? To which store to you enjoy going most often? What are your favorite pages in the catalogue? What home, car, vacation, or hobby do you fantasize about most? Do you have good health and satisfying relationships?

The things you desire most, bring you joy when you think of them, occupy your time, and for which you use your money are part of your path. Too often our students have told us they have always believed they could never really be, or do, or have what they enjoyed most. Somehow they became convinced that the concepts, people, and activities about which they were most passionate were also those most impossible for them!

Your passion is your path. If you like being with children above all other things, then doing something with children is likely to be part of your life's work. If you have the same intensity and passion for, say, sports, then something with sports is part of your path.

Know this. What you love to do most contains your life's purpose! By working in areas that fulfill you and excite you, by doing what you truly love, you will flow into your life's work and will not have to seek it. *It* will find you!

Many of us believe that in order to follow our passion or path we have to give up something first. Even though we loved teaching about angels above all things, when the angels told us we now worked for God full-time and were never going to have "real jobs," our first thought was, "Oh, no! How will we support ourselves?" Now we know that God supports us, but at first we didn't see how that could happen. We wanted "real jobs" from nine to five, and *then* we would work for God the rest of the time. The truth is, God supports our work every second of the day!

Another friend loves teaching fourth grade above all things. As she seeks her spiritual purpose she is afraid that what God wants her to do will not be as good or fulfilling as her teaching. God will not ask you to receive less than what you have now in order to do His work. He will take you to higher and better joys—never less. Your next step is always forward and better than you have been doing, sometimes even more than you could have ever dreamed possible.

By using *The Four Fundamentals* and the Balance Wheel, we began to really break down the barriers that had stopped us. In addition, now we have a better understanding of the specific areas in which we need angelic help and support.

Think of the times in your life when you have tried to make a decision before circumstances were right, or you were ready. You may have worried yourself into a frenzy. Then, on the day when the time was right, you suddenly were able to move forward with ease and without worry. What happened on that one "right" day that was different? Simply this. All the parts of the larger plan finally had come together and you were ready to make your decision effortlessly. At that moment you knew how *balance* felt.

SUZANNE'S STORY:

After living in Italy for four years, I returned to the United States. Even though I was glad to be here, I went through great culture shock, plus grief from leaving the people, place, and language I had grown to love. I was not sure what I wanted to do here, considering I had become a very different person while living abroad.

I asked my angels for a job that would utilize my gifts, skills, and experiences best, and where I could use the several foreign languages I had learned and loved to speak. The job had to be well paying, in a low-stress environment with nice people. I gave my angels a deadline of Friday of my second week back. I had to find a job quickly!

Thursday of the second week was a miserable day. I was down to my last $20. Although the angels had encouraged me all along by what I call "miracles of synchronicity," the stress of my job search was showing.

I was crying my eyes out in the bathroom of a personnel agency when a woman asked if I was okay. Through my tears, I explained my situation.

85

She suggested I attend a support group for job seekers being held there the next afternoon, which was the "second Friday" deadline I had given my angels. At the support group, a man told me he believed I was perfect to work for a company that produced and sold foreign language tapes.

I left the meeting and immediately called the contact person. It seemed that my résumé had been written just for this job, which was conveniently located around the corner from the support meeting.

My telephone rang on Monday with a request that I come in for a job interview. At the conclusion of the interview, I was offered the job—for which sixty other people had previously applied! My perfect job had found me!

I know there were no coincidences. What happened to me was simply part of a larger plan. Through it all, I knew I was being cared for and guided by God and my angels. In the past, I would have felt desperate and fearful from the beginning, not just at the odd moment. I knew in my heart I would find a job where I could use my love of languages. In this job, I get to use all of them, plus learn more!

One of the things I have learned to ask for is that the right people come into my life. On days

when I had no specific agenda and no real options, I went out and just said hello to everyone! By doing this, God led me to the right people who led me to my perfect job and later my perfect apartment. Life is full of miracles when I let go and allow the angels to guide me.

Each of us has a purpose in life which God supports 100 percent! Our birth is not accidental. We have been told over and over again that each of us has been chosen to do certain work, and to accomplish certain things while we are here on this planet. It's obvious that few people doubt this, because nearly everyone asks the three major "mission questions" at some time, "Why am I here? What is my purpose? What is my path?"

If these questions are so universal, and we had planned to do specific work before we were born, then why don't we remember what it is we agreed to do? Good question, and since the answer is different for each one of us, it is a particularly good question for *you* to ask your angel to explain to you personally, as part of your ongoing dialogue.

Angels exist to help us receive what we need and to do the work we have committed to do in our life. They have been waiting for each of us to *ask* for what we need to follow our passion—and to fulfill our mission—and they will continue to wait—*until we ask!*

Sometimes it may seem as though absolutely nothing is happening even though you know you are doing everything right. Be patient, this is just a period of waiting. Not every day feels like a spiritual A+ day. There is a "bigger picture" which we cannot fully see or comprehend now. Remember Suzanne's story. It demonstrates clearly that our needs are known by God, and that He has a divine plan to fulfill our needs fully, whether we know it or not.

AN ANGEL MESSAGE:

> *Dearest seekers,*
> *There is great wisdom surrounding you that can answer every question, define every movement, and lead you forward with no*

stress. You could flow easily from one part of life to another, with no conflict in relationships, no problems with abundance, and no worry of the future. But you have been given, by God Himself, the gift of Free Will, and Free Will was given to humans so you could take charge of your own lives, your own beings. Why? To perfect your soul, of course. If you remembered everything from the time before time, you would come into this world with no need to do any work at all. There would be no reason to be born. Life is a school. If you knew everything the day you started kindergarten, why even go on through the rest of the grades? If you knew all things the day you graduated from high school, why go to college or bother to learn a skill or trade? Your inner "memory" of what you want to accomplish and do leads you into your soul's growth and your life's purpose. There is sense in life, and that you do not remember your reasons for being born is part of the sense. Talk to us about it. We love to help you remember.

Our Daily Prayer

Dear God, Please bring
the right people, circumstances,
and events into my life today
that I may better do thy will.

Chapter 5

Praying for Yourself

In our survey, designed to identify the reasons our students believed that *The Four Fundamentals* would not work for them, we continually heard variations on a common theme. By far the greatest problem people have in contacting angels and in asking for angelic help for themselves is their limited beliefs and personal attitudes about their worthiness.

Beliefs That Limit Us

"I'm not good enough." At a low point in her life Barbara was in therapy. One day her therapist asked her to make a list of everything that was good about her, everything about herself that she valued. The list Barbara brought to the next session contained only one item, "I can hang wallpaper." It was the best she could do after days of worry and work on her list. Her belief in herself was so limited, it took many other therapy sessions for Barbara to realize that self-worth wasn't about what she *did,* but rather what she *was,* inside. Her list reads differently today.

It is hard to recognize the presence of our angels standing beside us when our self-esteem is low, when we think we don't count and that God doesn't care. It is almost impossible to hear their words of support, praise, and encouragement, or to receive the abundance they are anxious to give us. We are too busy listening to our own inner, negative talk.

"Minimums are good enough for me." This was said almost with pride, as if it were a virtuous way to think. This statement appears to be a variation on what we were taught as children. "Don't be greedy." "Leave some for the next person." "Don't be wasteful." "There are children starving in China," or wherever else something awful was happening which our parents could use to make us feel guilty.

It is unfortunately true that we attract to ourselves only that amount which we believe we can receive. This is *not* because the angels will bring only small amounts to us. Not at all. When we expect or ask for little, we receive little. We would not recognize a large gift as ours because we have neither asked for it nor expected we would receive it!

If you have been asking for a cheap secondhand car that is just enough to "get you around" you wouldn't recognize a *free* Lexus or Lincoln if it came to you. You would think it was meant for someone else and say, "It must not be for me, it's too good to be true." Or, "What's the catch?"

"People won't like me if God gives me too much." Our mother used to say, "You have had enough fun. It's time to stop!" God does not withhold anything from us. *We* limit ourselves! Parents and other well-meaning adults have taught us all kinds of limiting beliefs. For example, we wonder why some people don't succeed in sales who appear to be potentially successful candidates and possess all the right characteristics. Is it possible that parents who preached, "Don't ever talk to strangers," and, "Don't cross the street," have preconditioned the child, who is now an adult, to be fearful of making contacts or even talking with new people?

We look back to our childhood and to how our beliefs were formed and realize we passed some of those beliefs on to our own children despite our determination not to. The core belief system with which we evaluate situations, conditions, opportunities, and people is formed early in life. Perhaps this is why we are often more concerned about what *others* think about us, than how *we* think about ourselves.

If you were taught, in your early years, that "money is the root of all evil," you probably grew up believing that you could not be *both* spiritual and wealthy. Further, since no one wants to be considered evil, you probably believe that you would be a bad person if you ever received wealth. Carrying this concept one step further, you would not even *ask* God for money.

Too many of us think that if we ever actually asked for money, somehow there would be "hell to pay," it would be selfish, it would demonstrate a lack of true spirituality, compassion, and so forth. Is it our fear that we would become unacceptable to ourselves if we had wealth? We have become so accustomed to surviving the "difficult times" that we are afraid we won't know how to deal with money if we have it. Many of us consider this a true statement: "Be careful what you ask for because you just might get it." Why were we not taught to say: "Be generous in what you ask for yourself, because God has much to give you."

"Everyone else deserves more than I do." This is the ultimate statement of poor self-esteem. It takes a balanced person to realize that *you* are the most important—and deserving—person in your own life. No one deserves more than you do. God wants to give us everything. He loves each of us equally. Learn to love yourself and be more important to yourself. No one else was born for you. No one else pays your bills, eats your food, or has your chicken pox. And surely no one else is going to die for you. Think of the last time you had a toothache. Did anyone else come in and offer to have your root canal? Until these things happen, then *you* are the most important person in your life. If people aren't willing to die for you, they don't get to tell you how to live, either.

DARLENE'S STORY:

I grew up in a house with alcoholism, drug abuse, physical and emotional illness. For as long as I can remember, it seemed as though my physical appearance was the primary focus of my household. My parents were very good-looking people, and the fact that I could not meet their standards caused them great grief. It was devastating for me to hear as a small child, "You were such a pretty baby, whatever happened?" Not only was there no support at home during those years, I was also taunted at school for being too fat, too tall, or having bad skin. I was reminded at home that those things were all true.

Maybe my angels are like the parents I should have had. They are always there and they are supportive. Some days, when I really need them, I feel them crowd around me like a big, protective coat. I feel very special and loved. My friends have noticed my emotional and physical changes. I will never be a model, but now I like myself and have a very special guy in my life. My angels have told me that he will be my life-partner.

I admit I do feel strange asking for things like a car, a sewing machine that makes buttonholes, and to fit into a size 16 dress, but it is not because I don't deserve them. I fell into the belief that you should pray only for *big* things. Now I realize that, most of all, God and my angels want me to be happy in every way that I want to be happy also.

Every message from my angels is helpful. Every day is a new adventure. My life is not perfect but the angels have been helping me to work on forgiveness. I now have a peaceful acceptance of the path on earth I chose, and the assurance of their help to continue on my right path.

So, if you see a smiling, happy woman in the driver's seat of a Honda Passport, wave or beep because I have just told my angels to buckle up, and we're singing along with the radio.

Thinking Bigger

Why is it so difficult to *think bigger?* Are we afraid to be selfish? Everyone wants to improve their situation in life. We pray sincerely for our desires. When we do receive that for which we have asked, we feel we don't deserve it. There seems to be no winning. It is no wonder we hesitate to ask in the first place.

People with meager self-esteem worry most about being selfish. When you develop a positive concept, you will understand you are only taking care of yourself and your needs and that there is abundance to go around for everyone. As your self-esteem begins to improve, you will begin to notice how many good things are coming your way. You will realize that God does love you and you will recognize the signs of it. God answers prayers. He sends good things constantly.

Many of us use the "Let's Make a Deal" offer when we absolutely have to do business with God. Let's Make a Deal is the belief that we have to give something to God in order to receive something from Him. Some think a "fair" exchange will tempt God into giving us what we want. Here are several typical Let's Make a Deal offers:

- "If you cure my wife of cancer, I promise I'll *never* swear again."
- "If you help me get this house, I'll *never* ask for anything again."
- "If you let me have this job, I promise I will tithe" (or pray daily, or attend church every week, or do something for the homeless, or floss every day, or who knows what).
- "If I can only win this lottery, I'll give half of it to charity. I promise, God."

We try to make deals with God because we are full of beliefs that limit us. Beliefs that God doesn't really want to give us everything we need and He will respond only to our offers of a trade. We believe that only by bargaining with God can we get on His good side and enjoy the love, compassion, goodness, grace, and riches of God! What a silly concept! Finite man is offering to make a deal with an infinite God who will give man everything his heart desires by simply asking anyway. We must learn to think bigger. We must learn to think of a "bigger" God, a loving, giving, caring, generous God. But how?

Simple! Start with these truths which we believe:

1. Realize there is no wrong way to ask God for anything.
2. There is nothing too big for which to ask.
3. You never have to "give to get" or sacrifice to receive—from God.
4. Whatever you receive from God takes nothing away from anyone else.

Have you ever bought a new car that was a brand you had never owned before? If you are like most people, once you decided to buy that car you began seeing that brand, even the specific model you bought, everywhere, every time you went out. Thinking bigger is a lot like that. When you decide to entertain big thoughts about God, you'll see evidence of God everywhere. You'll see God working, providing, loving, caring, giving, and helping you everywhere you turn, through people like you, and with the encouragement, support, and even physical help of the angels.

Small gifts can bring you just as much joy and abundance as large gifts. How many times in your life are you going to ask for a house? Two times? Three times? Compare that with the hundreds of things God and the angels can help you with every day.

Here are some ideas of requests which may appear small to you but actually may be important or even vital. "Please, tell me what to say to Mary to support her." "Help me to be patient with the children." "Let me find everything fast at the store." "Help me not miss the phone call." "Help me find my earrings." "Help me find the right doctor." "Help me select the right vitamins." *Nothing* is too small to ask for.

But when you think bigger, the more abundance you will allow into your life, and the less worried you will be. When you ask for assistance from God and the angels, you are really asking to be freed from your own personal barriers. You become part of the connection everyone is truly seeking. All anyone really wants is to love and to be loved. When we feel we are, we are at peace and know there is nothing good that God would ever deny us even when it seems completely impossible.

TOM'S STORY:

I had a small consulting engineering business and was building it into a very nice company. My wife and I had built our dream house *ourselves,* our kids were doing well, and life looked very good. Suddenly, my largest client declared bankruptcy! The client represented a large share of our business and when he couldn't pay us, we couldn't pay our creditors. Our whole life changed instantly,

but the worst day was when the Internal Revenue Service came and sold everything at auction to help satisfy back taxes. Our home was eventually repossessed and we moved in with relatives.

My wife had a heart attack and became unable to work. I found several nice positions with major contractors, but when the project ended so did my job. For fourteen years, we lived like this: short-term jobs interspersed with long-term unemployment.

The IRS became our constant worry. Since we were in "tax trouble" we could not own property or get credit of any kind. We could not even have a bank account because any small sum of cash was subject to seizure by the government. The amount we owed continued to grow as interest and penalties added up and it seemed we would never resolve our difficulty.

Then we attended an Angelspeake workshop and learned to turn our tax problem over to God and the angels. We asked them to help us settle this mess and believed it would happen. We were able to let our negative attitudes toward the IRS go. For the first time we were not afraid. We felt the angels would take care of us and we didn't have to give our problem any more energy.

Through a friend, we heard of an attorney who was an excellent negotiator. Even though we had approached the IRS many times before, he assured us we could be relieved of the tax burden, which, by now, was $76,000. Within months an offer of compromise was accepted by the Internal Revenue Service for a negotiated amount we could afford.

The most miraculous gift was not the settlement, however. We believe the angels helped get us our loan money approved by a credit union so we could accept the offer. We had had no credit for many years but we were given the loan with no collateral! We are now making reasonable payments to relieve the debt and can see that we can finally own property and have credit again.

It may seem the IRS had changed its mind. But we know we were at an impasse. The only thing that eventually changed was us and our idea of the situation. The angels' help in doing that made the difference.

The Spiritual Self

God gave us a brain to use, but our brain is only a tool to help us with our life. Our brain knows how to run our body and store information, but it knows nothing about our purpose, path, or mission. Our brain sorts information and helps make most decisions. However, it does not have *all* the information we need to make every decision. If not, where does the rest of the information come from?

Within each of us is a spiritual self, which is a sense of "knowing." Some people call it their "soul," others their "gut." Whatever you call this sense, believe in its validity. The spiritual self guides us apart from our brain or mind. By combining mind and your spiritual self to make decisions, you will increase the number of successful choices or decisions you make in every area of life.

Our thoughts come from all of our past experiences and accumulated knowledge. If our experiences have been severely limited, we make uninformed decisions. We believe we all are doing the best we can in our relationships, business dealings, and life changes based on the information we have today. However, by combining our mind with our spiritual self, and with the help of our angels, we add the dimension of values to our decision-making process and we reduce the risk of making poor choices.

It is easier to raise our expectations as to what is available in life for us when we are not working under fear or pressure. By realizing we have a brain to sort information, an inner knowing to balance the spiritual and intellectual parts, and angels who guide us, we become much less vulnerable. We are in a much better position to make correct choices.

Still, there is no guarantee that we won't make mistakes. So what if, after all, you made a rotten decision? The plan for your life still exists. Your angels are still beside you, helping with the next event and the next decision, and the next, and the next. Expecting minimums will keep more *from* you than inappropriate choices.

AN ANGEL MESSAGE:

Dearest Children,

If we could give you a belief, we would give you this one. There are no limits. If after every thought or every prayer you asked yourself, "Am I limiting God's love for me?" you would understand much better as to what is available from Him. God has no limits! Limit not yourself. Believe in yourself. Believe that God believes in you.

A Buddhist Prayer to
the Triple Gem

I Seek Refuge in the Buddha

I Seek Refuge in the Scriptures

I Seek Refuge in the

Monastic Community

Chapter 6

Praying for Others and the World

Everything Is Everything

The angels tell us that we are so connected, that when a child is born, everyone is changed. When someone dies, we are all touched. When we pray for others, or love, or cry, we are sending messages that literally send energy and make a difference to everyone else. All of us on earth are connected and affected by every other individual in the world. Each of us is equally important and makes a difference. If you want to change the world, start first to change yourself.

Imagine having a thread coming from your heart that is attached at the other end to the person you love most. Imagine many other threads also coming from your heart that are attached to every person who inhabits the planet—and thousands more threads from their hearts attached to everyone else's. Can you begin to see how interconnected we are?

Think of all the threads that are connected to you which you know about. There are so many! But think of the ones you don't know about! When circumstances or events in your life occur which have no apparent connection and yet have a greater meaning, you are experiencing synchronicity. Some people call them coincidences, but when you understand how intertwined we all are, you can see that these happenings are only a momentary activation of connected threads. One event leads to another, which leads to another, which leads to yet another, and so on.

It is easy to see that our earth is ill and needs to be cleaned up and better cared for, but at other times it is difficult to see a personal kinship with the predicament our world is in. The angels also tell us we will not die if the earth dies, for we have an eternal soul which will continue. But if the earth ceases, the universe will shift and be less for the loss of earth's existence. God's plan has order. Earth is important because it is part of God's order and God has asked the angels to help us save this beautiful planet. We are all an integral part of God's greater plan for our world.

When you have an experience which seems like a miracle, look for synchronicity. Information of some nature is being passed from one person to another. When you read the stories of people who have written to us, look for unexplained, synchronous events. There are actually very few miracles in these stories. Look for the unexplainable in your own life. When it happens, it means that you are experiencing God and His angels at work. Everything has a greater meaning. The way we talk to God, or activate our thread to Him, is through prayer.

Praying

Someone said that prayer is when we talk to God and meditation is when He talks to us. However it works, prayer activates our direct link to God, and through this communication we are able to make changes in our lives, events, relationships, and circumstances. Prayer is Asking. But even more than that, prayer is Believing, Letting Go, and Thanking. A good prayer to God contains all four of the fundamentals.

Asking **in Prayer:** Acknowledge that God is there and that He will help you with your request for yourself or others.

Believing **in Prayer:** Give up personal concerns and doubts and believe that God is the one who can give you what you want or need. Believe God is listening to you and that your dialogue with Him is open and working.

Letting **Go** **in** **Prayer:** Stop holding on to whatever you are praying about. You release the whole prayer to God. It is like mailing a letter. You drop your communication in the "box" with total expectation and trust that it will be received.

Thanking in Prayer: Thank God for what He is doing, has done, and will do. Give credit to God and acknowledge His work in your life.

Praying for Individuals

———

It is good to pray for others. Here is the way our angels taught us to pray when we wanted something for someone else.

1. Love, love, love. Surround your request with love. Love is healing, comforting, and supporting. You cannot send *enough* love when you are praying for another person.
2. Ask for God's will to be done.
3. Ask for strength for the person you are concerned about.
4. Ask to be shown how you can help.
5. Ask for their healing in the areas of their greatest need.

Practice making care-giving statements while you are praying. "Dear God, please help Betty to do well today while taking her test." "Dear God, help me to be patient with my sick children." "Dear God, help Peter feel your love and strength while he heals." "Dear God, show me how to help my mother while she is dying." "Dear God, give me the strength to get through this day." "Dear God, help Joe wherever he needs it the most."

The energy of the prayer will serve as a healing tool for the body, mind, and spirit, wherever it is needed. Dr. Herbert Benson and Mary Stark, coauthors of *Timeless Healing,* offer scientific evidence that faith has helped cure medical conditions. Sick people who were prayed for recovered sooner than those with comparable illnesses who weren't prayed for even though the patients who recovered sooner didn't know they were the object of prayer. Praying for others is very satisfying. When you love someone and are concerned for their well-being, sometimes praying is all you can do.

Praying for Groups

We discovered that our students found praying for themselves more difficult than praying for others. Some thought it was selfish to pray for themselves, but had no compunction about praying for friends and relatives in need, or for unknown starving children in Africa. When we pray for others we feel connected to our world. As more of us activate our threads of energy with caring and concern about issues, more energy will be directed, and the greater the healing will be.

Many angels work only for world concerns, such as world peace, helping starving people, or saving the planet. In the last decade, we have seen some worldwide miracles happen that would have seemed impossible just days before they occurred. The reunification of Germany, and the collapse of communist Russia are only two of the most dramatic, unanticipated events. Millions of people had been praying for world peace. These two events alone went a long way to help world peace happen. Prayer works.

Refining Prayer

Whether you are praying for individuals or groups, it is important to remember that everyone has their own divine guidance. God and the angels are leading each of us into our best alignment. When we try to take over the personal lessons of others, we are literally playing God and only impede that person's progress. We never really know what another person's path or life is about. We get into the "God business" when we find ourselves fixing, controlling, or manipulating— even through our prayers. We may be aware we do these things in our daily life, but we may be unaware that we do them in our prayer life.

Many people do not understand the difference between care-taking and care-giving. Fixing, controlling, and manipulating are care-taking behaviors that strip people of their personal power and capabilities. Care-giving is empowering and allows people choices and opportunities to improve their own lives through their own experiences. Check your motives when you pray to be sure you are not trying to fix, control, or manipulate others—or even God.

If you aren't sure how to pray, just say, "Thy will be done." You can never go wrong with this uncomplicated statement. We find the more simply we express ourselves, the more balanced our connection with God. When you ask for something, just ask. Don't tell God or your angels *how* to do it or suggest ways you think will work best. Just ASK.

You, too, have your own divine guidance and if

you find people are trying to fix, control, or manipulate *you*, here is how we have been taught to deal with it:

You never have to *explain*.
You are doing the best you know how
to do today.
You do not have to *justify*.
You are doing the best you know how
to do today.
You do not have to *defend*.
You made your decision with the best
information you had at the time and . . . you are
doing the best you know how to do today.

Praying correctly was a big concern of our students. Here are some of the questions they posed to the angels:

Q: I expect the angels to know what is best for the world. How specific do I need to be?

Your prayer energy will never be wasted. Even if you should pray for something that cannot happen at this time, the energy sent will still make a positive difference to the people involved. Be as specific

as you know how to be, but realize that intention
and love are the most important parts of prayer.

Q: How can my one prayer make a difference in
the world?

Because, child, we are all one. The threads Trudy
and Barbara have told you about are much more
than energy. They are bonds of love, and healing,
and helping. This is part of faith. You may never
know how it can help, but it does. Believe it and
keep on praying!

Q: Is it possible for me to talk to other people's
angels and ask them to help my friends, or the
homeless?

Yes, yes, yes! But realize that others are being
protected by their angels, just as you are protected
by yours. Your prayer will be a gift of love, but
know their angels will do what is necessary to help
them from their more intimate point of view.

Q: Do I have to pray like my church teaches?

If you would like. Pray as your heart leads. It will
lead you well.

We can also do more than pray. When we put

action behind our prayers, then we really connect our loving heart with mankind. It does not have to be on a massive scale to make a difference. Teachers feel they can make a difference, one child at a time. You can make a difference one prayer or one deed at a time. Ask your angels for guidance as to where you can do the most good.

MARI'S STORY:

On December 7, I was Christmas shopping and *Angelspeake* was one of the gifts I purchased. The next morning, instead of wrapping all the presents as I had planned, I found myself reading *Angelspeake.* I didn't know how much my life was going to change within forty-eight hours.

Around 2:00 A.M. Sunday, I was awakened from a sound sleep, hearing music in my head. I thought, "Could this be my angels?" I started asking questions about the music. Then I heard, *Don't talk, listen. Let your head clear.* I became frightened and began to pray. They said, *Way to go!* Then I knew the angels were really there!

The next morning they woke me again with a song I recognized, "Love at Christmas." They said clearly, *Thousands of streets are full of hungry people. Feed the homeless at Christmas.*

The following day I kept hearing, *Call Barbara.
Call Barbara.* When she answered the phone, I
burst into tears! I explained to her what the angels
were telling me, and how upsetting it was to me. I
explained I couldn't possibly do what they were
asking because I worked in retail, my hours were
too long, and I didn't have the money to feed
homeless people.

She told me, "Angels don't give a direction like
that and not give you the means. Go back to them
and ask how you are supposed to do it."

One more time the angels woke me up, saying,
Pay attention. This is what you will do. They told
me to make stockings and fill them with a loaf of
bread, a can of tuna fish, peanut butter and jelly.
They said to put in a toothbrush and toothpaste, a
washcloth and soap. They said to help the homeless feel like children on Christmas morning and
put in an orange and a candy cane. I asked how I
was to do all this, and they said, *Ask for help.*

I'm not used to asking for help, but I didn't see
any other way. In the morning I started cutting
out huge stockings with pinking shears out of fab-
ric scraps I had around the house. The angels
were always there. Once, when I got a blister on
my thumb from the scissors, they said, *Don't you
have any oil?*

As I finished sewing a stocking, I would staple a card on it saying what was to go inside. My husband took a bunch of stockings to his work. He came back the next day and asked for more. I asked the people at the coffee shop for help and they filled all their stockings and asked for more. I asked my friends and everyone wanted to help.

Every night the angels would come to me. One night, exhausted, I asked, "Why do you wake me in the middle of the night?"

It's the only time you'll listen, they answered.

It was easy to get food for this project, but the toothbrushes got out of hand. I asked a company which sells toothbrushes to hospitals if I could have two hundred for my project. They supplied them at no charge, but must have misunderstood the number I wanted, because when I picked them up there were two thousand! I ended up giving toothbrushes to other charitable groups. The soap came from a hotel along with shampoo and hand lotion as well.

The stockings were coming back filled to the brim. Then, one morning I got the message. *Teach them to feed themselves.* I got permission from Trudy and Barbara to copy page 39 of their book, *Angelspeake.* I reduced the page to a 3x5 card and hung it on the outside of each stocking. I wanted people to know their angels could help them if they learned to **Ask.**

On Christmas morning, five of us met early and headed for the freeway underpasses. We found people all covered up, staying warm, sleeping with their shopping carts beside them. We left a stocking on top of each cart, along with a quarter and a note saying, "Please call home. Someone does care and wants to hear from you today."

Those who were awake shouted "God Bless You!" as we left. We found families, old people, and a young couple with a baby. We gave them blankets we had also collected, and in the end distributed over two hundred stockings. My goal was to touch one life. We touched more than one, and they touched us back.

This year we gave out over three hundred stockings to the homeless, plus the angels asked us to make special stockings for a local children's home. Then, we decided to expand our work. The homeless are in need 365 days a year, so we now serve breakfast every Sunday morning to those who come to the park where we distribute the food. I have returned to school and am completing my degree and am planning on becoming a minister. When the angels woke me up, they WOKE ME UP! I am deeply grateful they did.

AN ANGEL MESSAGE:

PRAY. PRAY. PRAY. Loving gifts of thought and healing will never be wasted. Prayer is activating your thread to God.

A Jewish Prayer
for Healing of Body and Spirit

May the one who blessed our
fathers, Abraham, Isaac, and
Jacob, and our mothers, Sarah,
Rebekah, Leah, and Rachel, send
healing to those in our midst who are
ill. May the Holy One have mercy
upon them. May they soon know a
healing of body, mind, and spirit
along with all who are ill.
And let us all say,
Amen.

Chapter 7

Praying for Miracles and Cures

Miracles are nothing more than God's will in action. There are miracles you ask for and miracles you don't have to ask for. We may see a miracle as an unexpected, extraordinary experience, but to God it's all in a day's work. There are natural laws of the universe and it may appear that miracles occur outside those laws, but truthfully, miracles just use laws we know nothing about—yet. If you had been alive one hundred fifty years ago, and had seen someone plug a wire into a hole in the wall, after which a piece of glass was illuminated, you surely would have believed you had witnessed a miracle.

Prayer is very much like plugging into an energy source and then using that energy for something practical. God hears our prayers whether we are praying individually for our own needs, or as a group for the larger, expanded needs of the planet. God's "blanket" of love and healing energy surrounds our planet, much like the atmosphere. Prayer is the way we access that energy.

One time we asked our angels, "What is God?"

They answered, *God is the glue that holds the atoms together.* Suddenly, we understood how encompassing God is. He became more understandable to us, even though we have been told over and over again that God is bigger than finite beings can ever imagine. We could also see that God is in everything if He exists between the atoms. The other day, our angels said, *There is not one person on earth who can even begin to come close to understanding what God is and what God does.*

All we really need to know is that God has assigned all the angels necessary to help us in any, and every, need. If you are seeking a particular cure or miracle, and really don't know which angel is the best angel to help you, ask God to send the most appropriate one. Specifically ask for a "Cancer Healing Angel" to help, if that is your need. Request the guardians of your children to protect them. The right angel will always come to you whether you ask or not, but for some there is a lot of comfort in asking for the presence and help of the "proper" angel.

Accessing an angel seems miraculous the first few times you do it, but soon you begin to feel as though you are speaking to an old friend and have no doubt an angel will be there whenever needed. One of the most amazing things to us about angel contact is that they are always there when you ask for them to come to you. You don't need a miracle to make contact.

If you can access an angel, you can also access a miracle. Angels bring miracles, too. How? There is no *new* news here. You Ask. You Believe. You Let Go. You Say Thank You. There is no difference in the way you ask for help in finding a parking place than in asking for healing for your pain, asking for protection on the highway, or asking for any other specific need to be met.

In one class, a woman became very upset when this was said. She asked, "Are you telling me that finding a parking place belongs in the same category as healing my husband's cancer?"

Obviously, the importance of requests is vastly different, but the formula is the same. A parking place is not a matter of life or death, but if you have practiced *The Four Fundamentals* on small things, you will have little difficulty in using *The Four Fundamentals* for big things.

This is when you need to Let It Happen. If a loved one is dying, and you have Asked for their cure, and truly Believed that God has the power to do it, then it is necessary to release the control to God—100 percent.

DONNA'S STORY:

My experience of working with God and His angels and asking for a miracle was far different than I anticipated and far more beautiful than I could have imagined. In June, my husband, Ralph, was diagnosed with pancreatic cancer and was told he would live for three to six months. We prayed for a miracle. Our family and friends prayed for a miracle. We wanted Ralph to be cured of his cancer.

At the time, I was learning a healing technique and I felt as though God had placed me on this journey so I could help Ralph. I helped him by using my healing gift to assist him with pain control and we were both confident he was improving. We felt blessed during this time and we enjoyed our days together. I was hoping the miracle had occurred, but I continued to pray.

In early October the following year, I could see that Ralph was no longer continuing to heal. He was having a lot of pain, and my angels told me the end would come soon. Finally he reached the point where he stayed in bed much of the time. I remember sitting on the edge of the bed, looking into his eyes and saying, "Honey, I am still praying for a miracle for you." Ralph looked at me with love and peace in his eyes and he said, "The miracle has already happened. You don't have to continue to pray." Ralph died on November 21. At peace.

———❦———

Donna prayed for her husband to be cured of cancer, but he died. Did she do something wrong? No. No. No. The miracle she asked for was a cure, the real miracle was he died in peace. God, in His wisdom, knows what the correct miracle is for each of us. Everyone dies and our angels tell us that the method and time of passing over is between God and the person who is making the transition.

By now you know that nothing is too big for God to give to you, or too small to escape His loving attention. Our intellect may agree with that, but how much do we really *trust* that a miracle will happen after we have asked for something and have immense feelings about the outcome? After you have *Asked* for the miracle to happen, and you have *Believed* it will happen—for the greater good, *how do you Let It Go?* Does it seem impossible? How can you let go of wanting the miracle that will save your mother's life, or your dad's farm, or your child's vision? How can you let go of the very thing you want above all else? Only a saint could possibly do that, and God knows, humans are not saints!

We want to let you know, you do not have to let go of the *thing* you have asked for so passionately. You only have to let go of the *wanting* of the outcome. Keep the passion for your miracle, because that is part of the love you feel. But as to *wanting* an outcome, let it go!

Please do not confuse letting go with not caring. When you Let It Happen or Let Go, you are allowing God to do His work. The more you hold a "want" to you, the less likely the miracle can happen, because you are keeping ownership of what you are asking for, and not giving your request to God.

Wanting is a barrier. Think of wanting as a fence. On one side, you are the supplicant, asking for a miracle. At the same time, you have created this barrier called wanting. On the other side of the fence is the result you requested. By releasing, or letting go of the wanting, you release the barrier that stands in the way of the reception of your request.

Wanting is lack. Wanting creates fear. It means you do not have and it means your attention is focused on what you don't have, rather than on what you desire. When you remove the *wanting* and start focusing on letting go, you can concentrate on the positive outcome you are seeking. Anytime you say yóu *want* something, you are pointing out that you don't have it! When we focus on our *want,* we are seeing the illness, not the cure. We are emphasizing the problem, not the solution. We are holding on to what we think is best rather than letting go. When we move out of the way, God can do His work.

So how do you release wanting? This is how we do it:

1. **Sit quietly.** It is not important to meditate or pray.

2. **Think** gently of your worry or fear and your "wanting."
3. **Find** the place within yourself that holds your fear. It may be your solar plexus, your neck, your back, your head, your heart. Scan your body to feel where the tension is as you think about your worry, fear, and/or *wanting*.
4. **Breathe.** Inhale, and when you exhale, relax the tense area in your body that holds your fear. Do it again. And again. Each time you will feel the burden of your fear and *wanting* release or begin to seep away from your place of stress. Each time, the heaviness will become smaller and smaller, until you find you are no longer fearful or worried at all.

Again, this does not mean you don't care. In fact, you will feel more free to help wherever help is needed. Fear is an enormous, incapacitating emotion. When the issue is released, the fear will go, too, and you will feel more empowered to solve the problem. Furthermore, because you have taken down the barrier of wanting, your request is no longer blocked. This leaves an opening for a miracle to occur.

This method of releasing the wanting of an outcome doesn't have to be saved for crises. Letting

Go is the way of attracting anything to you that you would like to have. Practice the technique we have outlined and learn to use it whenever you feel blocked from receiving all that God has available for you.

We begin our prayers each day by saying: "Dear God, I offer myself to thee." We have then released to God the outcome of every act and event during the day. We don't always know what is best, but we know that God does and we start the day by turning everything over to Him.

Trudy's youngest daughter, Katie, was diagnosed with juvenile diabetes when she was thirteen years old. Although it was a time of fear for everyone in the family, it also became a time of praying, releasing, and turning over to God. When Katie went off to college, Trudy knew she needed to start releasing the *wanting* to control Katie, her diabetes, insulin injections, food, and everything else connected with her daughter's college life! Trudy soon realized the only way she could get through this was to pray and ask God and Katie's angels to care for Katie and help her stay healthy. Trudy found her fear in the pit of her stomach and released her *wanting* every time she recognized the fear returning.

Katie's work-study program at college required her to find a part-time job on campus. The first job she saw on the list of "Jobs Available" was with a doctor who headed diabetes research at Boston University Medical Center. Katie called, got the job, and has learned more about diabetes and how to keep herself healthy than she had ever known before.

To Trudy, this was a grade-A, first-class miracle.

Prayer works. It just may not happen to work exactly like you think it will or expect it to. We have seen healing happen in many ways: as a result of prayer, through touch, through positive thought, even through a chance meeting. And in some cases, spontaneously.

When healing energy is present, anyone in the

area can tap into it. When there is an opening, God sends healing to everyone present who needs it. Many times something miraculous happens for *you*, while you are busy praying for *someone else!* Often, the healer is also healed.

LINDA R.'S HEALING:

This is an account of my experience of healing that took place at an angel workshop I attended. I want to share my feelings and what has happened since.

I remember feeling very comfortable about the whole experience that afternoon. Everything we did seemed to come very easily. When everyone came together in a circle for an ending prayer, we were asked if there was anyone who had a health issue they were dealing with. We were asked to stand in the center of a "healing circle" so the group could pray for them. I didn't hesitate. I had been suffering with a muscle spasm for two weeks which was causing me a great deal of pain. I had experienced it in the past and it always required several doctor's visits for a very uncomfortable procedure.

I entered the circle not knowing what to expect. I remember focusing on a woman named Joan who was also facing some serious health issues. Standing next to her, my own pain seemed insignificant. Even though I asked to have my pain healed, my attentions were mostly on Joan. At the closing prayer, which focused on healing, I felt an energy go through the group as well as through me. When the prayer was over and all hands released, we seemed closer than before.

I left that day unsure as to what had taken place. The following day I realized the pain from my muscle spasm was better, but not enough to get excited about. By the end of the week, the pain was completely gone and the pain is still gone! I am delighted.

I must tell you at this point that I consider myself to be a levelheaded person who does not "buy into" things easily. I cannot be certain that it was healing through the angels. However, I can tell you this: never before has this agonizing spasm gone away without an enormously painful medical procedure. It has kept me from doing many things, and at one time forced me to quit my job.

I would like to believe there is an angel watching over me. I am still a bit unsure of what I feel, but I am closer to being a believer. If I have an angel, I know it is a true gift from God that my pain is gone.

AN ANGEL MESSAGE:

Dear Ones,

God will take your worries, concerns, fears, and pain if you let Him. He has His hands out and His heart is willing, but you must let go. We hear your cries saying from the innermost reaches of your soul, "God, what more do you want from me? What more do I have left to give?"

And God answers you with love, "Give me your pain. Give me your fear." And you know that you cannot. For your greatest fear is that without pain you would be nothing.

God says this to you: "Dear child, Wherever you think you will be less by giving to me, you will find more. I will replenish you, glorify you, and enhance you. I will not take away and leave you lacking. That is not my way. I give. I love. And I heal. That is my way. I have miracles for you. Make room for them."

A Christian Prayer

Our Father who art in heaven,

hallowed be thy name.

Thy kingdom come, thy will be done,

on earth as it is in heaven.

Give us this day our daily bread and

forgive us our trespasses as we

forgive those who trespass against us.

And lead us not into temptation, but

deliver us from evil.

For thine is the kingdom and the

power and the glory forever.

Amen

Chapter 8

Coping with "Misses," Doubt, and Anger

⊹⊶⊷⊹

If you are having difficulty connecting with your angels, it might be the *wanting* it to happen that is getting in the way. Simply *Let Go,* and begin writing whatever comes to your mind. Rarely do students *not* receive a message from their angels in our classes. However, when readers are trying to learn to communicate with their angels through a book, it can be a little more intimidating. Perhaps one is more secure and less doubtful with a group's support.

A Letter from Mark:

The approach in your book seems too simple and too effortless. I would like to know if attending your workshop will help, since I am still stuck with the approach in your book. Or will your PBS video benefit me beyond what is in the book?

I think I know my "destiny" and my strengths. What I'm looking for is that angelic guidance and help to get *to* my destiny. Right now I am flying blind and deaf and would really like to be in touch with God and my angels. Can you help?

Mark is receiving messages. He wants more proof and thus intellectualizes his experience. He doesn't need more instruction. Angelic communication comes through the heart . . . not the head.

Christy's Story:

I went to your Angelspeake workshop last Sunday and really enjoyed my time there. I wish I had the words to tell you how much your book/class touched me.

I seem to have difficulty communicating. I have asked my angels to speak with me and to help me hear them. I feel/hear them early in the morning. I know it's them because I feel comforted. I am aware I'm asking them questions and that I am getting answers. It's all like sort of a dream . . . but not.

When I am totally awake, the good feelings are still there, but my questions and their answers are gone. I have no recollection of answers or questions except an incredible feeling of comfort and joy, which is great, but I need more. *As I am writing this I've decided it might be kind of important to ask them to help me understand what is being said!?* Well, that's a thought! I'll try that.

Thank you for your time.

Christy is more open to her angels in the morning because she has not yet started "thinking." She is more available to angelic communication. During the day, her brain engages and she begins to question the messages she receives. We were delighted to read in her letter that she had solved her own problem! The words in italics are actually an angel message she received. She asked for more and received more in her next thoughts. She is receiving just fine.

Here are some of the more common reasons people feel they are not receiving messages:

1. **I don't hear them.** People expect to hear actual words spoken into their ears. It rarely happens

that way. There is simply a
sense of knowing what to
write. The message is not
in your brain or ears first,
but rather in your heart
first. Just begin writing
whatever comes to you.
Many students tell us that
if they refuse to write what
comes to them the message is
continually repeated until they
write it down. Others say if they don't write what
comes to them, nothing further comes through
until they start writing again.

2. **I still think it is me making it up.** The fact that
you think you are making it up is proof you're
not. You do not question whether you are writing a letter or a grocery list. Just write, set it
aside for a day or two, then reread your message. Can you tell the difference between *your*
writing and that of the angels?

3. **Why can't I just keep talking to them in my
head?** You can. But you will get more pro-
found messages and teachings when you write
them down.

4. **I get the most boring messages.** We have had
those periods, too. Sometimes there is just not

much going on in our lives. This is when you can ask a question. Sometimes your angels will lead you into a great topic through the questions *you* ask.

Here are some thought starters for you:

What do I need to change in my life?
What would you like to teach me today?
Tell me about God.
Who can I help or support today?

5. **I don't <u>feel</u> my angels anymore.** As you develop spiritually, you become more integrated with the angels' energy. At first, you were in one place and the angels were "out there." Later your energy and theirs became less separate or distinguishable from that of each other. The fact that you cannot *feel* them so clearly now is evidence of your progress.

6. **Are we worshiping angels?** Once when we asked this question, the angels just laughed and laughed. They said, *No prayer could ever stop with us, for we have no will to create anything. We can only do what God gives us the power to do, each and every time. Even if you tried to worship us as you would God, the prayer would just go right through us to where it belonged. Right to God's heart.*

141

When Friends and Family Doubt

It is terribly disappointing to have the wonderful experience of angel communication come into your life, only to have no support from your family or to discover that they look at you with patient tolerance. Many people are so fearful of God that their fear is translated into fear of anyone who talks with God or any divine being, including angels. Barbara has a friend who escapes to her car whenever the subject of angels comes up.

We believe it is important to have a close connection with a spiritual buddy or a group of spiritual people. Angel contact is exciting! The desire to share our messages with friends can be very strong, so surround yourself with like-minded people, and, for the moment at least, leave your skeptical family and friends out of angelic discussions. They are entitled to their own beliefs.

The worst, however, is when you have someone in your life who thinks that angel contact is evil and warns you repeatedly that bad things are going to come into your life to hurt you. Don't be surprised that this type of person will think you are mistaken and have gone off the deep end, and pray for you. Angels never judge, scold, preach, or give advice, and we aren't supposed to either. Angels tell us that everyone has reached where they are today through their own need to be with God in their very own way. They also say that we are exactly where we are supposed to be today. If there is no one else in your life who believes in angels, then *you* be the first one in your family to believe. Thank the person who is trying to fix you for their concern. The angels do not have to be "sold" to anyone, nor do they need apologies. They make contact with people when invited, or when the time is perfect. Remember that not long ago you might have thought people who talked with their angels were a little batty, too.

When PBS stations across the United States began to broadcast *Speaking with Your Angels: A Guide,* our special Angelspeake program, the positive reaction was overwhelming. We did receive a few phone calls from people who were concerned about our message and the state of our souls. Rather than argue about the content of our program, we accepted their thoughts and "blessed them on their way."

When we say a prayer and ask the angels to be

with us, we are no more at risk of being bothered by negative energy than when we pray for God to come with His love. Our prayer asks that we be covered with the love and light of God. One must invite negative energy in and be open to it to have it come to us. Asking works both ways. If you ask for good, it will be there. If you ask for negative, you will find it!

The angels have told us that when we pray for protection, they surround us with their love and that they are a secure source of information. If it worries you to talk to angels, or it goes against a belief you have established, then communicate with God. Angels are God's messengers and will do the work God desires in any event. A comfortable connection is the most important thing.

When the Message Seems Wrong

Early in our angel communications, Barbara's angels told her she would be meeting her perfect partner in August. Barbara hasn't had a decent August since. On occasion, you will receive a message that doesn't come about as the angels promised. We have learned that the angels did not lie to you and will not play games with you.

CATHY'S STORY:

It was recommended to me by a spiritual friend that I purchase your book and follow its teaching to connect with my angels for personal guidance. It was so simple to write my angels, and I loved the messages I received. I had decided to resign from my job with a six-figure income as a vice president of a major real estate company. I desperately needed validation that I had done the right thing by removing myself from an extremely negative environment. I was convinced that there must be a successful company out there that operated more ethically. For months I had been contacted by headhunters wooing me for positions that were of interest to me, and I resigned with the belief that my new job was just around the corner. The angels assured me I would be employed by October 1 at the latest.

Well, October 1 came and went. Still more assurances. I decided the beautiful responses to my queries had to be coming from a part of my own conscience that was responding to my own wishful thinking. My friend explained the difficulty spiritual beings have with time frames. I couldn't believe my angels would be inaccurate when they certainly understood the importance to me of their being on target! I was so upset with my angels I refused to communicate with them further and then I tried to reach Trudy. It's a good thing we didn't connect for several weeks, because when we finally did talk, I was a lot calmer and in a better frame of mind to receive her advice.

She suggested I buy the book *The Game of Life and How to Play It* by Florence Scovel Shinn. I sat down to browse through it in anticipation of reading it later, when I opened the book to the page with a passage that reads, "When a man can wish without worrying, every desire will be instantly fulfilled." Oh, brother! Have I just been hit over the head with a message, or what?

I am a corporate executive, a wife, and the mother of four children. I am used to solving problems and responding at a moment's notice. It's hard to turn full circle and simply wait for higher beings to do their thing in their time frame.

Well, here I am—waiting, networking, waiting, sending résumés, waiting, second-guessing myself, waiting, worrying, and waiting. I know in my heart of hearts I will be employed in a wonderful new job. My lesson, obviously, is to trust God. Everything will come to me when the time is right.

If the information from your perspective was not right, focus on what was and go forward into all your new options. There is so much available to you that is good, exciting, and positive, there is no need to look at what you missed. You are offered more now than you can imagine or know.

We asked the angels why some messages seem wrong, and were told:

We say, give it time. Give all messages time. Often, when we give you a prediction of an event, you think it will occur within the next day or two. Sometimes this is true but more often there is no scheduled moment for anything to happen. Synchronicity of events governs the agenda.

Flow. Flow. Flow. This universe is governed by law. Every single thing in the universe is moving outward from the center point, which is the genesis. If something does

not happen as was predicted, then know
something better came up. There are choice
points in everyone's life where they decide to
go forward in one direction or to choose
another. Your Free Will is to be used to decide
what to do next. You have many alternative
options available. If you married another per-
son, or had followed another career path,
would you have a different life today? Yes.
The Four Fundamentals work <u>with</u> Free Will,
not alone. Your lives are not preordained. It is
not fate as to how you end up.

You are in the process of creating your
spiritual life. You made all your choices
today by flowing in the best way you could.
All others in the world will be affected by
your choices. One choice affects all because
we are connected, each and every one.

Angel Messages You Don't Know What to Do With

Sometimes you will receive information while receiving a message you don't know what to do with. For example, one time Barbara received a message for a woman named Julie, whose story is in *Angelspeake*. Julie was very ill with cancer but was still in the process of chemotherapy. The message was loving and comforting, but since Barbara had never met Julie, she didn't feel comfortable just mailing it off to her. The message was too wonderful to ignore, so finally Barbara decided to mail it to Bob, Julie's father-in-law. Barbara gave Bob permission to pass on the angel's message at the most suitable time. Later, when Bob knew it was right, he gave Julie the message and she was grateful for it.

In deciding what angelic information to share, we ask ourselves, "If I give this information, will it improve or enhance the situation?" If the answer is yes, we share the angel messages when the time is appropriate. Otherwise, we don't.

When we decide to open to the angelic realm and ask for information or guidance, we can't ask in a qualitative way. It is unacceptable to say, "Okay, angels, tell me only the good information. Don't tell me anything I won't like." We are not going to receive half a gift. If we are going to be open and available to the angels' teachings and information, we must also be ready to hear love and truth of all kinds. Angels give us only the information God directs them to.

When All Seems Lost

There are angels for every part of life's drama and circumstance. Trust that you are being supported in every way.

KRISTA'S STORY:

Looking back, I knew my son had died the day before he was born. On October 2, I was nine months pregnant. I felt terrible and my stomach was a hard ball. At 2:30 in the morning, I woke up ice cold and I was shaking uncontrollably like I was in shock. My breathing was erratic and difficult and it was as though every difficult breath I took was also his last.

The next morning my doctor did an ultrasound and when there was no heartbeat, the doctor said, "We've lost the baby." The technician began to cry. My husband was called to come and be with me while they induced labor, and our son was born about 6:20 P.M. on October 3. We discovered the umbilical cord was wrapped around his neck two times. I delivered little Eric in silence with no first cries of life and with no birth certificate to sign. I was pulled with wanting to live for our other children and wanting to die just to be with my little one.

After Eric was delivered, I felt an incredible lightness of my own body, and I immediately mentioned this to our chaplain. I felt so light, like I was being physically held up and given strength and comfort. The room was also bright and it felt like a sanctuary. I could honestly feel the warmth and peace inside the room in spite of all the metal equipment and the rushing medical personnel. There was an indescribable peace and lightness.

The day after Eric died was our tenth wedding anniversary. I came home with empty arms on what should have been a day of double celebration. Over the next few days and weeks I felt a sense of strength and comfort that could only have come from "the other side." Even though my grief was enormous, I believe with all my heart a hedge of angels and loved ones who had died surrounded me during my lowest points in the hospital and when I came home.

There have been two experiences which have happened to me that have let me know that Eric is in the room with me spiritually. Both times, I was feeling overwhelming emotions of sorrow which were replaced with feelings of unconditional love, and I knew immediately that there was a sending of love from my little boy and comfort from my angels.

I had prayed so hard during my pregnancy that our baby would be healthy, and while the memories are intensely sad, I have also experienced a peace and comfort that was sent from God. It softens the pain of remembering. Even though it may seem my prayers for a healthy child were not answered, this time has been very special and pure. It is difficult to tell others my story because I don't want to lose the meaning it has had. But I want you to know of this time, and I hope you can understand.

Grief is not a feeling we enjoy, but it is an important part of your healing. There are angels who receive the departing soul into heaven, and who make sure the transition is comforting and without fear. We can only assure you that there are angels of comfort who come to the bereaved soul who is still living, and they do what is necessary to help them get through the difficult time. Angels weep with you.

When You Are Angry with God

When we feel betrayed by anyone, it takes time to renew the friendship. If you are angry with God, your relationship with Him needs to be healed. When life has been hard, unfair, or painful, it was not God who hurt you. It was another human being who used their free will in a way you could not understand. If your car was stolen, you wouldn't rage at the manufacturer. Know that God did not let you down.

Occasionally we hear comments like these, from people who are really mad at God:

"I'm so mad at God I can't believe He would give me anything."
"I never received anything I have ever asked for in the past, so why should it be different now?"
"After all that has happened, I'll never trust God again."
"I prayed and prayed and He never answered me."
"How can there be a God when He did this?"
"If God is so loving, why did this happen?"

No one escapes life's troubles or lessons, but everyone can find help and healing in prayer. If you need to, yell at God. Tell Him why you are mad at Him. Scream. Shout. Cry. Release the energy concerning your anger with God. Then ask for His help. It has always been there. It always will be there.

God doesn't make bad things happen to people. Every event of your life is part of your learning. There is a bigger plan at work. Don't give up your faith. Everyone is exactly where they are supposed to be, no matter how awful, unfair, or painful it may seem. You didn't do anything wrong or pray inadequately, no matter what events occur. We will never be able to figure out God's greater plan. It is beyond our comprehension.

Ask, Believe, Let Go, and Say Thank You for understanding, patience, and strength for yourself and your loved ones. Look for the miracles in terrible times. But most of all, look at how you are never alone.

AN ANGEL MESSAGE:

Dear Children,

When it seems that all has been lost and there will never be joy in your heart again, look for the good. Look for the good in every situation because it is always there. When the worst is upon you, so is the best. And how can good things be happening when you are sitting beside the bed of your dying child? Look away from the child. Look at the friends who surround you. Look at the support you are being given. Look at the faces of those who mourn with you, and know that no matter how lonely you feel, you are not alone. And if there is no one else there, look for us. We do not just support the one who is dying, we are also supporting those who must stay on earth and finish their tasks.

God never gives ugliness or hurt. Agony is already within the human condition. God brings strength, joy, and love. Look for it always. And please, children, look for us, for we are the ones who will deliver God's help to you. We are showing ourselves to you in many ways. When you are crying in the darkness we are beside you caressing you and loving you. You truly will feel us. Read, again, our beautiful poem, "Angel Touches," for we are always there.

A Child's Prayer

Now I lay me down to sleep.

I pray the Lord my soul to keep.

If I should die before I wake,

I pray the Lord my soul

to take.

156

Passing It On

⊢•▰•⊣

We would never have thought to ask for all God and His angels have given to us. And we are still being told by our angels, *The best is yet to be.* After *Angelspeake* appeared on the best-seller list, we were told there would be another book, built upon the information foundation of the first book. There would be more and deeper information forthcoming and we would have no trouble with content. In fact, they said, *The second book has already been written.* We found the second book had already been written, because it was your stories, letters, experiences, and questions which created *The Angelspeake Book of Prayer and Healing.* The angels say there will be more books. Sometimes a miracle is so big, we can't even tell when it is unfolding. We are all in the middle of a miracle.

We were looking for the "secret to the meaning of life," and our angels have shown us there is no secret. Everyone can find out whatever they need to know at any time! If we have learned any secret, it is only the knowledge that God and His angels are always there. Not a very well kept secret!

We have learned to let go and allow the angels to do what they do best. They see the "bigger picture," which we certainly don't see and no longer have any need to see. Our angels handle all the details. We can ask for something, but we have found the angels give us better than what we asked for and more than we could ever imagine. Our limited human minds do not understand the generosity of the universe or the enormity and goodness of God. As the angels tell us, *On earth, humans say, "You owe me more," In heaven, God and the angels say, "Forget the change."* We are learning what it means to say, "on earth as it is in heaven." They are showing us how heaven works, and then they give us explicit examples! We have also learned these gifts are not unique to two sisters from Iowa. They are completely available to everyone!

We love your stories and meeting you as we

tour the country giving seminars and classes. Our Website is www.angelspeake.com. Send us your stories and experiences. The angels work with you and also through you. When you find people who love angels, teach them how to Angelspeake. When you find people who have lost hope and their hearts are hard, ask God to soften their hearts and to heal them with hope and love. Pass on what the angels have given to you. This information is to share.

A FINAL ANGEL MESSAGE:

Children of Everywhere,

You are already working for God. Miracle after miracle has been plunked down in your path as proof we exist, and still you doubt. But as you do the work God desires you to do, you will realize God works through you. If you even say "maybe" to us, then we can begin. God loves you so much, He has created a heavenly kingdom of angels to help you find Him. The true miracle is God. We only tell you what God's message IS. Our message is God's truth. We are there in the stillness. We are there in the waiting. We are there in the knowing. Just BE. We are there.

. . . Believe It!

About the Authors

Barbara Mark and Trudy Griswold, sisters and coauthors of the widely acclaimed *Angelspeake: How to Talk with Your Angels,* are internationally known teachers, spiritual counselors, and angel experts. Their Angelspeake seminars have been featured on of many national television and radio programs, including ABC's *Good Morning America,* CBS's *Leeza Show,* and FOX's *Good Day New York.* Public Broadcasting stations around the country are showing *Speaking with Your Angels,* a PBS-produced video of an Angelspeake seminar. Barbara maintains a private practice in San Diego, California, and Trudy maintains her private practice in Westport, Connecticut.

You can communicate directly with the authors on the Internet. Their address is http://www.angel-speake.com.

29839167R00094

Made in the USA
Lexington, KY
09 February 2014